FIRE SISTERS RISING

Overcoming the Impossible to Achieve the Extraordinary

CHARLIE CARDIN

For information contact :

Fire Sisters Rising, LLC
11010 Lake Grove Boulevard
Suite 100-113
Morrisville, NC 27560
www.FireSistersRising.com

ISBN : 978-0-9982086-0-2

First Edition : October 2016

Dedication

This book is dedicated to my brother.

Clinton Cheval Wofford

Born: December 9, 1968

Died: September 2, 1983

He had a smile that would melt hearts, could give hugs that would heal your soul and he had enough ambition to light the world on fire.

He was my protector, my hero and my friend and he will forever light my fire to empower those that have lost their way.

Acknowledgments

I want to express my deepest gratitude to all the people in my life who have been there for me to support me and love me and be my cheerleader even when I struggled to cheerlead myself. For privacy, I leave names out, but you know who you are and words cannot express the gratitude that I feel toward each of you.

To one special woman, Sandi Showalter, who helped me with editing parts of this book. Sandi has been my friend since Elementary School and has seen me through some of my most difficult times. I am fairly certain that I would not have survived my childhood without the love from her and her family. There is a deep love between us that is unconditional and it will forever span time and space. She is my sister through and through.

To my mother who taught me the power of resilience and to my stepfather who taught me how life is all about maintenance and how important it is to show up for the people you love.

To my husband and two boys who fill my life with light and love every day, and they give me the fuel to march forward to do my part to make this world a better place for all.

Preface

I lived through unimaginable abuse for too much of my life. It started in childhood at the hands of my father and continued through relationship after relationship, including two failed marriages. But this book is not just about my story and my struggle; it's about helping you with your story and your struggle. It's about providing the tools, techniques, and strategies that can transform your life. It's about your moving beyond just surviving to becoming the ultimate survivor.

In order for me to move forward toward a life full of passion and purpose, I had to find the lessons in my experiences. My hope is that sharing these stories may inspire you to process and let go of the pain of your own experience. If you are reading this, you have survived or are working toward survival. No matter what type of adversity you have endured, you are here.

Getting here, however, was from easy. Families commonly hide abuse. During my journey I discovered that earlier generations of my family had hidden atrocities that helped shape who I became. My family was notorious for covering things up. They told me to get over it or that it just wasn't that bad. While I am living proof that you can get over it, I will never tell you that it wasn't that bad. I also won't tell you to cover anything up. As I have learned, "getting over it" meant finding a space for me to speak about my abuse. That allowed me to heal and stop letting it control my life. Openness, healing, and taking back control— this is what I want for you and for all survivors.

So many of us enter the vicious cycle of abuse through no fault of our own. We remain trapped there because we know nothing else. We learn how to carry the secrets and not disclose them so that we appear normal. We become experts at covering things up. This tragedy persists because many believe that abuse is a way of life, and they continue the cycle for most, if not all, of their lives. Sometimes they don't even realize that they are being abused.

For those who finally do break free, they face an uphill battle because society tells survivors that once they are out of an abusive relationship they should be fine. Reality proves that the long-term effects of abuse influence families everywhere, carrying through to multiple generations.

Survivors like you and me need to tell our stories. Ever since I founded Fire Sisters Rising, thousands have reached out to me. Many are still suffering from the effects of abuse even though they ended the abusive relationships years ago. They have shared story after story of how the abuse impacted themselves, their children, and even their grandchildren. Some force themselves to stay single because they have given up hope of ever having a loving relationship. Others resolve to remain alone due to fear and shame.

That is why I'm writing this book to give you strategies to reframe and reprocess your own impossible situation, so that you can free yourself from the weight of what has happened. It is then that you will step into your own extraordinary life, a life on your terms, using your wisdom to help yourself and others in positive and empowering ways.

This book concentrates on celebrating our survival and that of many others to come. We can, and we will, rise together from the ashes of our stories and step into a life of freedom, a life of compassion, a life in which we are ready to accept and reciprocate love.

CONTENTS

My Story

Loss and Responsibility

"Suicide doesn't take away the pain. It gives it to someone else."—
Author Unknown

My brother Clint and I sat crouched in the closet. His arms were
wrapped tightly around me, and I couldn't stop crying. My father had
come home drunk. Again. He started chasing my mother, all while
yelling at her and landing blow after blow. My mom was hysterical, and
my father was simply crazy. Furniture was broken. More importantly,
souls were broken.

It wasn't just my mother he decided to make his victim. My father
abused my brother and me repeatedly. He manipulated our whole
family. We weren't even teenagers yet when he offered us drugs. My

mother was shattered, both mentally and physically, and sat by powerless to stop it all.

Then my father left us to be with another woman. His departure freed my mother from her abuser, but she lost herself completely. Although she lived with us in our house, my brother and I were left on our own struggling to survive it all. And for a while we did, barely, until my brother succumbed to a life of drugs and alcohol.

In the summer of 1983, when I had just turned 13 and my brother was 14, my mother became desperate to break Clint's addictions. She delivered him to a friend's farm in Arkansas, where he changed tremendously. Clint was beginning to love life again. He had escaped from our father's abuse, from our mother's powerlessness, and from the reality of the war we lived through every day at home. When we returned to pick up Clint, he spoke of this being the happiest time of his life. His days of working on the farm, tending to cows and horses, and bailing hay gave him an immense sense of peace. I saw a glimpse of what he could be and felt how different he was once free from the drama of our home life.

But it wasn't to last.

After returning back home to Florida, Clint quickly reconnected with his old crowd and former addictions. He went right back to his previous life in the war zone. Once again there was no one there to protect or guide either him or me.

Within a few short weeks of his return, one morning before school Clint was storming through our house, upset that he didn't have a nice t-shirt to wear. He and my mother were screaming at each other before he abruptly left. The fights were always bad, but I knew that this time something was different. I walked to the bus stop reluctantly, dragging my feet as though each shoe weighed 100 pounds.

When I returned home from school, it was raining heavily. It was the kind of rain that engulfs you in seconds and makes you feel as if you were drowning. I had worried all day about my brother, so the rain didn't faze me. All I knew was that I had to find him. I roamed the streets of the neighborhood, knocking on door after door and asking, "Have you seen Clint?" The answer was always "No." By the time I made it to my best friend's house two streets away, I was soaked to the bone and shivering. She took me in and gave me a towel and something to drink. We strategized on where else he could be and made phone calls. Everyone said that they were sure he would turn up at some point. Finally, I was forced to give up my search and go home.

After a restless night my father arrived to take me to a weekend party. I put my fears aside and went along to escape the deep sadness I was feeling. It seemed so odd to me that I was leaving the house without my brother. He was my protector, my hero. Even in the darkness of our life together he would always bring a smile to my face and a warmth to my heart.

Two days later while I lay sleeping my father came into my room and started speaking to me. At first it seemed as though all sounds were muffled. I struggled to open my eyes. My father's lips were moving, but in my sleep-fogged state I could not hear what he was saying. My father's girlfriend was hysterical, and I looked at her trying desperately to understand what was going on. Then slowly the fog started to lift as I heard my father repeating again and again, "Clint's dead."

I didn't know how to feel or what to say. I just sat there numb, letting the waves of this horrible truth wash over me. Those two words echoed inside my brain, slashing at my soul like a knife. How was it that the only person who understood or loved me was dead? How could somebody so alive, so much a part of my world, suddenly be taken from my life?

My father explained that my mother had found my brother's body in the woods next to an electrical tower. It was the same tower he had climbed a thousand times, the same woods where we had camped and played and swum in the river, the same place where we had immersed ourselves in nature. Our sacred place. Our place where all that mattered was that moment in time and where the heaviness of our life disappeared. Our place that was now, suddenly, just my place and would forever remind me of a life taken too soon.

The next few days were a blur, but I remember with crystal clarity when the police came to the house. They reported that based on their analysis Clint had jumped and committed suicide. It didn't surprise me because I had thought of suicide myself so many times.

As the realization sank in that my brother was gone forever, I became lost, completely and utterly lost. The pain was too much to bear. I found myself wishing that he had taken me with him. How was I going to survive alone? There was no one now to care for me or love me or protect me.

My father kept telling me over and over, "You have to be strong for me and your mother. There is nothing compared to losing a child." This mantra translated into, "Your feelings don't matter, and you must take care of us." It was during this time that I realized just how much I had already taken care of both of them for my whole life. I didn't question my father's assertion; I simply accepted the responsibility as I had been trained, and I did what I could to help them get through the memorial service and the ensuing days.

My Story

Falling Victim

Long before my brother's death, in fact as young as I can remember, my father used to bring me to sketchy bars and nightclubs in Florida to watch him perform music. I grew up thinking that it was perfectly normal for people to reek of cigarettes and alcohol. I thought nothing of patrons exchanging drugs and money. I watched, and I learned. I learned that barmaids knew exactly what to do to earn an extra tip. They were my teachers on how to whisper in a man's ear. I had a front row seat for their lessons on the importance of showing a little skin.

I turned into a confidante for many of those barmaids, a listening ear for all their troubles. Even though I was very young, they would tell me about sex, money, and drugs. No topic was off limits. My father encouraged such interaction because he was always entertained by how easily people would befriend me. He indoctrinated me in how important it was to always be there for anyone who needed me. He programmed me to believe that my beauty and spirit were bestowed upon me only to serve others.

Nothing is more important for a child than pleasing her or his parents. This is not an area where children have a choice, and I was no different. I didn't realize that my father was preparing me from birth to fulfill his desires. He always felt that it was his right to touch me whenever and wherever he wanted. He conditioned me to believe that such touching was out of love. He taught me that this is what I was put on this earth for. I believed him. I trusted him.

My father was incredibly gifted as a musician, and he had many devoted fans. They would follow him to all of his shows, and I got to know these people very well. He would parade me around, telling all the drunks and drug addicts, "Isn't she beautiful? Don't you wish she were yours?" A few of them convinced my father that he should let them touch me. He'd give me a long story about their broken lives and how a little gesture like allowing them to touch or kiss me would give them a glimmer of hope. He preyed on my compassion. He capitalized on my unconditional love for humankind.

One night, when I was 14 years old, what little innocence I had left was shattered. It was around 4:00 a.m., and my father had long since passed out after a long night of playing music, drinking, and partying. I was entertaining myself by daubing my father's toes with a beautiful red nail polish. As I painted, one of his friends was chatting me up, repeating some version of "Oh, you are so pretty. How about you give me a massage?" I complied as usual. After all, my father had told me that this was my job as a woman. I finished the massage and got up to make my way to the bathroom. I was in there only for a fraction of a second when the door opened. I knew what he was there to do. He was twice my size, so there was no way I could fight him off. I let out screams for my father, but he didn't hear me in his stupor. As his "friend" violated me, my father's words played over and over in my head: my body was not my own; it was only there to serve whomever deemed it worthy.

I told no one. I had no idea that this was wrong. I mean, it felt wrong, but I didn't know that I could speak up, and I didn't know whom to tell. The whole episode was just a confirmation of what my father had conditioned me to believe for my entire life—namely, that my feelings didn't matter and that my body was not my own.

My Story

Becoming a Survivor

The abuse did not end with my father and his friends. Soon it was my first real boyfriend pulling me by my hair across a parking lot. He seemed to relish beating me, that is when he wasn't verbally and sexually abusing me. He worked hard to destroy every last shred of confidence I had. He was extremely skilled at convincing me that the abuse was my fault, a strategy I would later learn is called "gas lighting." It was two years of unrelenting abuse before I found the courage to make it stop.

My father had conditioned me well because, even though I had left my first boyfriend, the abuse continued with one after another. The worst experience occurred in my third year of college when a handsome and charming man picked me out of a class of a thousand. Despite

everything I had been through up to this point, I still believed in and blindly trusted people. Little did I realize that he was a predator and that I was his next conquest. Predators know how to locate their prey; they can sense weakness from across a room and go in for the kill.

After the first date he said that he had fallen in love with me, and I believed him. When he got extremely jealous if I talked to someone else, he said that meant he cared about me, and I believed him. When he started spreading rumors about me, he told me that it was to protect me from other people who wanted to take something from me, and I believed him.

My friends told me that something wasn't right; they advised me to break off the relationship. Of course, I didn't listen. He had me convinced that he would give me the world, so long as I didn't do anything to make him mad in any way.

The physical abuse started slowly—slapping me on the face, throwing things at me, kicking me out of the car to make me walk home in the dark. The incidents still weren't enough to make me leave him, though.

Then one day we went to visit his mother. He told me that he had to take care of some business and left me alone with her. While he was away, his mother told me stories of the many times he had tried to kill her. She told me that the business he was there to "take care of" was a court appearance for two felony charges of theft against him. Her words penetrated through to me. I was numb and knew I needed to leave, but I didn't know how I would escape his grasp.

I played it cool all the way back home, but I started secretly to plan my escape. I knew that I had to get away during a time when he would be at work. I didn't mention a thing to him, and then the day arrived for me to set my plan in motion. As soon as he left, I had a friend meet me at the apartment, and we quickly started packing, but within twenty minutes my boyfriend returned home. I don't know how, but he had figured out my plan.

He was enraged and started throwing cans of food at me. When he ripped the phone out of the wall, I screamed to my friend to go to a payphone and call the police. While she was gone, he dragged me by my hair to the bathtub, beating my head against its rim. Then he dragged me back to the living room, got on top of me, and put his hands around my neck. I knew that I was seconds away from taking my last breath. Then, suddenly, the police were there. He released his grip, and I gasped for air. I was free.

It wasn't quite over, however, because even with a restraining order in place he stalked me. He left messages on my car. He called my friends and parents and told them that he would kill me. The police advised me to find a safe house. That's when I relocated to my mom and stepdad's house on the beach where, fortunately, he couldn't find me.

I had survived again.

I wish I could say that was the end of the abuse, but I can't. Now, instead of a boyfriend's abusing me, I had graduated to my husband's doing the same thing.

In my first marriage the mistreatment again started slowly with mind games and then sexual abuse, but to the outside world we looked like the perfect couple. After he and his friends drugged and raped me, I found the courage to end the marriage. It took me two long years to divorce him. I was so lost and broken, and I had no idea of what a healthy relationship looked like.

The cycle was not over when I entered my second marriage. My new husband had three sons whose mother was in jail. I felt that I could save them all. Unconsciously my powerlessness to save my brother was transferred to saving these boys. This driving force blinded me to the dangers of the man I had married. The reality was that the three boys' father was an alcoholic. Shades of my mother and father played out again—that is, until I got pregnant.

Then everything changed. I realized that I had a fire within my innermost being. It had been there latently for a long time, but I had ignored it.

While I was used to abuse, I wasn't going to let anyone hurt my child. Suddenly it wasn't just me. I had a miracle growing inside me. I experienced a love so overwhelming, so unlike anything up to that point in my life, that I found the courage I needed not only to face the harsh reality of my second marriage but also to decide to break the cycle forever.

I divorced my husband. I put an end to abuse in my life and in the life of my child.

I won't pretend that it was either easy or quick, but it was necessary.

My Story

The Journey toward Freedom

"Nothing ever goes away until it teaches us what we need to know."—
Pema Chodron

One fundamental shift that changed everything for me was the
realization that I would continue to be given the same lessons over and
over again until I retained what I needed to learn. It is only then that I
could fully open myself to the possibility that things could be different.

I don't have to tell you, especially if you are a survivor, how frustrating
it is to go through one abusive relationship after another. The messages
that my father had given me since birth were powerful and played out in
my mind repeatedly. They were reinforced with every failed relationship
and every abusive act. The messages had convinced me that there was

something wrong with me. I believed what all of my abusers had told me. These were men who I thought loved me, but instead they had taken advantage of me, abused me, and even tried to kill me.

My biggest breakthrough came when I realized that what I thought of myself shouldn't include the opinion of anyone else. Once I fully accepted that truth, it freed me to allow self-compassion and forgiveness. I forgave myself for all the bad decisions. I fully accepted that my actions had been based on information I had at the time. I shed every last comment by anyone who did not have my best interests at heart.

Throughout all my previous relationships I had let others lead me wherever they wanted. No more. I was determined that this was the end of that pattern for me and my son. Although the conditioning from my childhood was strong, I was on a mission to change it completely and forever.

As I learned to take care of the life growing inside me, I learned how to take care of myself. I realized the true extent of my love and gained a respect for myself that I had never experienced earlier. Through the loving care that I showed to my son, I began to care for myself. After he was born, the unconditional love my son displayed toward me made me realize that love is not supposed to hurt. For the first time in my life I learned that love was about giving and forgiving, about happiness and strength.

The inner fire I had recognized was just beginning to ignite.

I was determined that I would never get into another abusive relationship. My therapist told me, "If you feel a really strong attraction to anyone, run the other direction," and I kept that counsel front and center in my mind. For two years I dated here and there, but mostly I focused on my healing and growth. I discovered the work of Tony Robbins and listened to his "Daily Magic" constantly. I focused on my personal growth and on my son.

I journaled, I processed, and I did craniosacral therapy. I did every single thing I could to reverse the programming ingrained in me since birth. One of the most important things I learned was how to reframe the events that I had been through to release the pain while keeping the lessons associated with each event.

As I started to reprocess these events, what became clear to me was the true measure of courage and strength that I possessed. I realized that even the most horrible events had taught me something.

What I learned from my early exposure to drugs, for example, is that I had developed incredible life skills while navigating bars and dealing with drunks and drug addicts. As I watched, firsthand, how both my father and brother got sucked into the world of hard drugs, I had seen what they could do to a person. I vowed never to fall into that trap and never to risk my life that way. This was a valuable lesson to have under my belt when I went to college. I was able to reject drugs when a lot of my friends didn't or couldn't. I witnessed too many people throwing away their scholarships and futures for an unsustainable high. I would never let that happen to me.

My rape also taught me the danger that arises when drugs and alcohol are involved. I stayed mostly sober during college parties. I knew that to protect myself I needed to stay alert and aware.

My early conditioning to please others developed into an incredible strength. When I started working, I took whatever job was offered so that I could cover expenses. I even helped my mother pay bills. This work ethic eventually led to my joining Junior Achievement (JA) during my junior year in high school. This wonderful organization taught me how to run my own business. It was exhilarating, and I busted my butt to win recognition as Achiever of the Year. This honor allowed me to attend JA's national convention in Indiana. In my senior year I became president of my company, which was voted Company of the Year.

The experience with JA cemented the lesson that the power to please can turn into an unrelenting passion to succeed. Junior Achievement showed me that no tragedy in my earlier personal life had any bearing on what I could achieve in business. I carried that passion forward to graduate from college and pursue a career in technology.

My safety zone was my work. Despite whatever was going on in my personal life, I found solace in my ability to succeed in industry. Hobbies were also a refuge. In college I competed in bodybuilding and bicycle racing. In addition, I found charitable causes like Habitat for Humanity and Shriners Hospital that surrounded me with good people and restored my faith in humanity.

More than anything, my success in work taught me the power of independence. Having the skills and resources to succeed allowed me to depend on myself rather than relationships as a measure of self-worth. It also fulfilled a deep sense of responsibility to my brother's memory.

My brother hadn't lived, so I had to. It was like the situation in The Titanic when Rose went on to fulfill the dreams that she and Jack had planned together. My brother and I had dreams of the future, and I was determined to succeed in memory of him.

This determination served me well throughout my corporate career. I worked hard, harder than most, and I took jobs that others wouldn't because the challenge never bothered me. My resilience, born of necessity, always carried me through. Whatever I faced in the future could never be worse than what I had survived in the past.

I would rather try and fail at something than let someone else tell me what I am capable of. The truth is that people don't know what they are capable of until they try. When I detect judgment or cynicism from others, I know that they are simply projecting their own apprehensions onto me, and I refuse to let someone else's fear guide me. I refuse to deny myself the right to make my own life extraordinary.

My Story

New Beginnings

"Authentic love does not devalue another human being. Authentic love does not silence, shame, or abuse."—Brooke Axtell

When I made the decision to end abuse in my life, I spent a great deal of time thinking about the type of person with whom I wanted to share my life. Equally important, I thought about the type of man I wanted to father my son. I made endless lists of all the qualities that were non-negotiable, like honesty and integrity. I wanted to be with someone who was independent, not co-dependent. I wanted to be with someone who would show unconditional love to my son and me.

That someone appeared in May of 2009. We met at a Buddhist meditation group, only to find out that we worked at the same company and in the same building. We decided to start getting together for lunch and learn each other's likes and dislikes. I learned of his failed marriage in the past and of his love for dinosaur excavations in Montana. For the first time in my life a man was genuinely interested in having a conversation with me. It was light and fun, and for the longest time I thought he just wanted to be friends.

After about six months of enjoyable lunches he asked, "Maybe we could meet outside of work sometime?" I enthusiastically agreed. I then knew that our friendship was turning into something much more. Through him I learned the power of deep connection and authentic love. He taught me what it felt like to be respected and adored. Most importantly, he showed me the value of honor.

I didn't realize how important a quality honor is in a man until I met one who had it. It is a trait that all of my abusers lacked and that we as a society are not instilling in boys. The man I had finally found knew right from wrong; he valued life and held himself to a high moral standard; he kept his word when he made a commitment. When he chooses you, he will protect you without hesitation or reservation.

I had never met anyone who valued me so much. It felt so natural to fall in love with him. We were married in January of 2010 at an intimate gathering in New Hampshire, and a year later we decided to add another member to our family. We both were so excited when I became pregnant with a second son.

No words can describe the joy in my soul after freeing myself from my past and creating an amazing life with my husband. There is no drama, no heaviness, no jealousy, no rage, no alcoholism, no drugs, no sadness. Instead there is only happiness together.

The only reason my past matters now is to record the value of my lessons and share them with the world. It is also to remember those I have lost.

This has been the story of my journey from abuse victim to survivor, from suffering in silence to speaking out, from continuously repeating mistakes of the past to discovering new beginnings and a new life.

The RVM Framework

for Change

Three Steps to Freedom

"Daring greatly means the courage to be vulnerable. It means to show up and be seen. To ask for what you need. To talk about how you're feeling. To have the hard conversations."—Brene Brown

Step 1: Recognize

The first step in making any change is to recognize what needs to be different. They say that recognizing that you need to change is half the battle, and that was proven true in my experience. When I finally decided to stop the cycle of abuse in my life, I knew that it was time to focus on peeling back the layers inside myself. I knew that it was time to view myself honestly and compassionately. I had to do it for myself and my son. I knew that if I didn't do this work I would never be able to experience the joy and freedom that I craved.

It was hard to look at the decisions I had made throughout my life. It was hard to admit them to myself, much less to anyone else, but I found the courage to challenge every single belief I had about who I was and what my life could be. During my two years as a single mother I learned how to take ownership of and responsibility for my personal life. I learned to accept that the fact everyone makes mistakes and that I didn't have to punish myself for them the rest of my life.

I questioned things like my compulsion to achieve at work and my ability to shine in business. I realized that was what gave me a sense of worth amid struggles in my personal life. I could hide everything when I was at work. No one cared or asked about my personal life, and that was just fine with me. I found a space where nobody except me defined what I was capable of.

I kept digging and challenged every belief I had formed about love, acceptance, and forgiveness. I knew what needed to change, and I knew that I couldn't do it alone.

Step 2: Vocalize

The second step in changing is to vocalize the struggle to yourself and to people who can help. I had gone through most of my young life thinking that if I talked to people about my struggles I would be judged and ostracized, so I kept silent. Throughout most of high school I let my sadness about my life consume me.

As the abuse continued, so unfortunately did my silence. It had become a survival mechanism to live in a fantasy that the abuse was not that bad. I did not want to tell the truth about it to my friends and family. I was consumed by shame and didn't want them to intervene. At the same time I felt powerless to control my life, my mind, and my body. Believing for so long that people just wouldn't understand kept me from telling my story and getting the help that I needed. I was in desperate times, searching for answers.

When I broke the cycle, I knew that I no longer could remain silent. I had to reach out to people who had hurt me and forgive both them and myself in order to grow and change. I had to confront the shame. I had to find people and groups and books to learn stories of others who had tough journeys and come out victorious.

I had to expose my vulnerabilities by telling my story so that I could heal and be whole again and fully integrate my experience into my life. I had to understand that my story and my struggle were part of my fabric. Whatever had happened was for a reason, and I became stronger because of it. I am not afraid now to share my story. I am not afraid anymore to be seen for who I am. I know now that I am not perfect and that perfectionism was a survival mechanism for me.

By reaching out to others and being vulnerable, I acquired courage. I realized that I had to vocalize not only to others but also to myself. I challenged myself to embrace being vulnerable. As I searched for and found people with whom I could be vulnerable, gratitude and joy flowed into my life. Allowing myself to be vulnerable with people who loved and supported me gave me an abiding connection to life.

Step 3: Mobilize

The third step in effecting self-change is to mobilize, which means to act in ways that will heal and promote freedom. I realized that it was far more difficult for me to recognize and be honest about what needed to change than it was to change. Once I understood why I needed to change and found support to help me, performing the change itself seemed easy. I just had to decide that the change was no longer negotiable.

Taking action has never been my problem. Ever since I started working at age 14, I have always been known as the GSD (Get Shit Done) girl. There are, of course, many other synonyms such as perfectionist and overachiever. Being a GSD type was my survival mechanism. I would not be alive right now and here to tell my story if I had not been able to find something in my life at which I could succeed consistently.

I had worked on different areas of personal growth by the time I was ready to take a really hard look at myself. The therapists who helped me the most focused on moving me forward and gave me techniques that worked. The ones who kept me trained on my past I didn't spend much time with.

Throughout this book I will share a lifetime of lessons learned during my journey and the important mindset shifts that helped me to free myself from the chains of abuse.

The fact is, however, that all the personal development techniques in the world won't work if you don't do the work. You need to mobilize yourself and start taking action to claim the extraordinary life that you are meant to be living. It starts with the first step. The only difference between you and any other person who has been successful in overcoming the impossible is your ability to take consistent steps forward. You don't have to pressure yourself to do everything in this book at once. You can do an exercise a week or every two weeks. First give yourself time to heal. I know that this stuff can be hard to look at. I know the pain and the sadness and the fear. But I also know that when you get to the other side it will all be worth it.

Are you ready? Can you commit to making maybe one change a week? One change a month? What will it take to get you motivated? How much longer do you want to be paralyzed in your shame and fear and repeating the same patterns? How much longer can you wait to move toward an extraordinary life? All it takes is a firm decision followed by persistent action.

In order to have lasting change and break the cycle of abuse forever, you need to perform the three steps of recognizing, vocalizing, and mobilizing over and over again to challenge every one of your beliefs in every area of your life. It is by challenging these beliefs that your mindset will shift, transforming your life to one of deep connection, tremendous gratitude, and abundant joy.

Lesson 1

Why do Abusers Abuse?

"Only an abuser can make the decision to stop abusing."—Ted Nugent

The primary reason for abusive behavior is to gain power and control. Abusers often have high self-esteem but many deep-seated insecurities that they project onto their victims. They feel entitled and think that they should have whatever they want when they want it. They think that having power and control over another is their right as a human being.

The abuser will do anything and everything to maintain that power and control. If he senses any threat to this control, the abuse will intensify. This is when extreme jealousy, rage, and physical/sexual abuse most often occur. Abusers are nearly incapable of true empathy, and they believe wholeheartedly that the victim's actions are intended to hurt them in some way. In their mind, by being abusive, they are simply protecting their own identity and feelings.

Abusers depend on their ability to create fear in their prey. They will vary the type of abuse to keep their victims off-balance. Maintaining a constant fear is their most effective ploy to ensuring control over their victims. Many times this need to instill fear in others is an attempt to displace the fear that they themselves encountered during childhood or in some other traumatic experience in adulthood.

Abusers' perception of reality is skewed. Their fears control how they process situations and relationships. When drugs or alcohol are added to the equation, the fears and the abuse most often intensify as well.

How Do You Know If You Are Being Abused?

What is your intuition telling you? You don't need a checklist or a book or anyone else's opinion to tell you what you feel inside. I encourage you to trust your intuition and then consider the following types of abuse as defined by the Centers for Disease Control and Prevention.

Physical violence is the intentional use of physical force with the potential for causing death, disability, injury, or harm. Physical violence includes, but is not limited to, scratching; pushing; shoving; throwing; grabbing; biting; choking; shaking; aggressive hair pulling; slapping; punching; hitting; burning; use of a weapon; and use of restraints or one's body, size, or strength against another person. Physical violence also includes coercing other people to commit any of the above acts.

Sexual violence is divided into five categories. Any of these acts constitute sexual violence, whether attempted or completed. Additionally, all of these acts occur without the victim's freely given consent, including cases in which the victim is unable to consent due to being too intoxicated (e.g., incapacitation, lack of consciousness, or lack of awareness) through their voluntary or involuntary use of alcohol or drugs.

o Rape or penetration of victim—This includes completed or attempted, forced or alcohol/drug-facilitated unwanted vaginal, oral, or anal insertion. Forced penetration occurs through the perpetrator's use of physical force against the victim or threats to physically harm the victim.

o Victim was made to penetrate someone else—This includes completed or attempted, forced or alcohol/drug-facilitated incidents when the victim was made to sexually penetrate a perpetrator or someone else without the victim's consent.

o Non-physically pressured unwanted penetration—This includes incidents in which the victim was pressured verbally or through intimidation or misuse of authority to consent or acquiesce to being penetrated.

o Unwanted sexual contact—This includes intentional touching of the victim or making the victim touch the perpetrator, either directly or through the clothing, on the genitalia, anus, groin, breast, inner thigh, or buttocks without the victim's consent.

o Non-contact unwanted sexual experiences—This includes unwanted sexual events that are not of a physical nature that occur without the victim's consent. Examples include unwanted exposure to sexual situations (e.g., pornography); verbal or behavioral sexual harassment; threats of sexual violence to accomplish some other end; and/or unwanted filming, taking or disseminating photographs of a sexual nature of another person.

Psychological aggression is the use of verbal and non-verbal communication with the intent to harm another person mentally or emotionally, and/or to exert control over another person. Psychological aggression can include expressive aggression (e.g., name-calling, humiliating); coercive control (e.g., limiting access to transportation, money, friends, and family; excessive monitoring of whereabouts); threats of physical or sexual violence; control of reproductive or sexual health (e.g., refusal to use birth control; coerced pregnancy termination); exploitation of victim's vulnerability (e.g., immigration status, disability); exploitation of perpetrator's vulnerability; and presenting false information to the victim with the intent of making them doubt their own memory or perception (e.g., mind games).[1]

Does your partner often act jealous or possessive?

Blame you for his behavior?

Control your money or access to a car, a phone, or the computer?

Destroy or take personal things from you?

Isolate you by forcing you to cut off contact with people you love?

Manipulate you, put you down, try to control you, or force you to do things that you don't want to do?

Text or call you repeatedly when you are not with them?

Threaten or physically harm your children or your pets?

Threaten to harm himself to convince you not to do something?

Threaten or physically harm you in any way?

Treat you like his property?

Try to convince you that the abuse did not happen?

If any of these questions resonates with you, recognize the type of relationship you are in. What changes do you need to make? What resources or plans do you need to have in place to make these changes? What would it feel like not to someone ever treat you like this again?

LESSON 2

Why did I Let Myself Be

Abused?

"Losing yourself in loving another can make you forget that you're special too."—Author Unknown

Nothing that you did or could ever do warrants abuse. You did not let yourself be abused.

Often, when looking for a partner, we seek out someone who possesses the skills that we lack. Because social messages convey that we are not enough by ourselves, we search for someone to complete us—someone to give us a balance of traits and talents such that, when together, we feel as though we are enough.

Abusers radiate an abundance of confidence and power that is incredibly enticing. If you look back to when you first met, it felt magnetic, didn't it? Your abuser used calculated tactics to attract and eventually control you. The "honeymoon" stage of the relationship can be amazing. Abusers shower you with gifts and compliments and promise you the world. They sense your insecurities and figure out how to make them all melt away. You feel on top of the world, as though all your prayers have been answered, but your abuser is manipulating you into becoming dependent on him.

When the abuse starts, it is usually slow. It comes in the form of snide remarks, putdowns, and humiliation in front of friends and family. Abusers will manipulate the same insecurities that they exploited to build you up to now break you down. You will be left wondering what happened to cause the change. You will ask yourself questions such as "What did I do wrong to make him do this?" or "What is wrong with me that he doesn't love me anymore?" This is all part of the abusive strategy.

The abuser will give just enough love and adoration to keep you thinking that there is a possibility of getting back to the "honeymoon" stage. If you fall for his ploy, you stay in the relationship. You may get married, have children, and give up everything for the chance of having back the person with whom you fell in love. Then the abuse gets worse.

Survivors can sense if the violence will get worse if they try to leave. When survival instincts kick in, a woman may stay in an abusive relationship because she fears for her children or be convinced her abuser will kill himself or have no financial resources to get out. When a survivor is living through such trauma every day, it can feel impossible to change the status quo.

I have talked to so many survivors whose families had patterns of abuse that extended over multiple generations. In these families there is often an unspoken belief system that "You are only as worthy as the women before you." We get stuck with the feeling that we don't deserve to have a better relationship than our elders had. Add on cultural expectations, and it can feel as though women have no choice.

There has been increasing pressure on women over the years to do it all—to help and to serve regardless of how we are treated. This pressure militates against our standing up for ourselves and following our own intuition and moral compass. We fall into a pattern of doing what people expect of us for fear of falling out of grace with societal values.

I distinctly remember a conversation with my mother when I decided to leave my second husband. She liked him. He was a charming guy and a talented carpenter. My mother told me to try counseling first. "Give it another try," she urged, so I did. He showed up drunk for a couple of the sessions and made up excuses on why he couldn't be at others. The ones he did attend, however, allowed my counselor to gain valuable information about the type of person he was. When I met with my counselor alone, she said, "I normally try to figure out how to keep people together, but I can't morally and ethically do that in this case." I knew that it was time to make a plan.

The decision to leave was the hardest of my life. I do not take my responsibilities lightly. I had made a commitment not only to my husband but also to his kids. I had tried so hard to help. But when my daycare worker reported that my husband had shown up to pick up our son after drinking in the middle of the day, I knew that there was no more time for thinking. I knew that my son's life depended on my ability to act. I decided that it was time to heed my intuition, to put aside whatever anyone else thought and do what needed to be done for our well-being.

What first attracted you to your abuser?

In what ways did he initially make you feel as though you were enough?

What feelings did you avoid by staying with your abuser?

What do you now wish you had done differently?

Is there anything that prevents you from doing things differently the next time you come into contact with an abuser?

What will it feel like when you no longer have abuse in your life?

What actions do you need to take right away not to be abused again?

LESSON 3

Giving Up the Dream

"A healthy relationship will never require you to sacrifice your friends, your dreams, or your dignity."—Mandy Hale

I have talked to hundreds of survivors who even after years of being out of an abusive relationship still thought that they could have changed their abusers. Usually such conversations started with "If only."

- If only I had stopped doing the things he didn't like. . ..

- If only I had loved him more. . ..

- If only I had had a better job. . ..

- If only I had lost weight and looked better. . ..

- If only I had controlled the kids more. . ..

- If only my family had been more accepting. . ..

- If only I had had friends he liked. . ..

The list could go on and on. This is the hollow "If only" dream to which many disempowered victims of abuse cling. It comes down to one simple truth: it is easier for a survivor to blame herself than it is to blame her abuser.

Survivors will do everything in their power to avoid the painful reality that an abuser does not care about his victim but only about himself.

Survivors who are still holding on to the dream will say, "But look at all the things he did for me. Look at all the times when we had so much fun together. Look at how well he treated me every time after he abused me. He would not have been able to treat me like that if he didn't love me."

Let me repeat: the abuser does not care about the survivor. He cares only about himself and his ability to maintain power and control. It's always all about the abusers. Every time they abused a woman partner and then reactivated the "honeymoon" period, their objective was to subjugate the survivor once more to their power and control.

Society blames the survivor too in saying, "Why don't you just leave?" "If you had more self-confidence, you wouldn't have done this to yourself." "It's your own fault. You shouldn't have dated that person."

The messages conveyed to women from birth are that they are not enough. Look at the messages in the media that focus on the perfect body, the perfect family, the perfect marriage, the perfect life. These messages set women up to doubt their self-worth and self-confidence. Abusers can detect with great accuracy in which area a woman feels that she is not enough. Abusers know exactly what tactics will build women up and then exploit their weaknesses.

The start of one of my abusive relationships happened in college when I was an avid bicycle racer and bodybuilder. I didn't know it at the time, but he told all his friends that he would marry me one day. He had already set his sights on conquering me. When he moved out of state, we stayed in touch for years and then met up when I was on a work trip in the state where he lived. He completely swept me off my feet. He told me how he had been in love with me for years; he told me all the things that he could provide for me. I fell hard and fast.

I ignored all the warning signs of sexual abuse when they started. I felt that it was my duty to comply with him. He exploited all of the weaknesses that I had shared with him years earlier. He knew what I had been through with my father, and he calculated exactly what he needed to say and do so that I would fulfill his desires. I thought that he cared about me, but he cared only about himself the entire time.

It was incredibly hard for me to accept this fact. I tried to convince myself that the abuse was my fault. I must have asked for it, I thought. How could he not care about me? His friends reached out to me and told me it was my fault. Even some of my own friends said the same thing while commenting that "You guys seem like the perfect couple."

How many times have you seen stories in the news about women who were abused or killed by their husbands or boyfriends, and friends who are interviewed say they had no idea what was going on? Typically, they add, "They looked like the perfect couple."

ow that abusers will continue their cycles of violence again and again. The only way to stop their power and control over you is to get out of the relationship. It doesn't matter how much you may love them; they will not change.

However much you may pretend that your relationship is something it's not, it will not change the fact that you are being abused. You can't change their behavior, and you are not responsible for them. You can't save them. The sooner you recognize and accept the relationship for what it is, the sooner you will be on the road to freedom and to living your own extraordinary life.

What dream do you need to let go of that is not serving you well?

How is holding on to the dream impacting your ability to move on with your life?

How does holding on impact your ability to be joyful and grateful?

What will it feel like when you give up this dream and accept the reality of the situation?

What is keeping you from giving up that dream?

Lesson 4

Releasing Shame

"Shame needs three things to grow exponentially in our lives: secrecy, silence, and judgment."—Brene Brown

When we feel shame, it is not for what we have done, or for a particular behavior, but for who we are. When we feel shame, we want to hide; we feel that we don't deserve love or respect. Shame is often a pervasive experience that we don't recognize. Shame can feel quite "normal."

When we feel ashamed, we emit a certain aura/vibe/energy. Others who pick up on this energy may misinterpret it and assume that we have behaved badly, causing them to overreact and us to believe that we deserve punishment. We may not recognize the ways we evince our shame and wonder why others are so hard on us. This is how others mirror our beliefs about ourselves.

I talked to no one about my rape or my father's sexual advances. I was paralyzed by shame and a fear of judgment. I felt that if I shared this experience it would uncover the full extent of the game my father had played with me, and I idolized him. I didn't want him to be hurt.

He had told me often what happens to kids who tell. They lose their families, their homes, their friends. I didn't want that to happen to me, so I stayed silent and did what he said. I lived for his approval and acceptance. I lived for the times when he told me I was enough.

Abusers feed on shame. It is through shame that they can implant the message in the survivor's mind that she is not enough—not skinny enough, not skilled enough, not pretty enough. Abusers are incredibly skilled at identifying and exploiting these vulnerabilities. The consistent message of unworthiness along with a dose of fear ensures that the survivor will never feel empowered enough to leave.

Survivors become trapped psychologically as shame takes over. They become consumed by worry and fear that their abuser will leave them due to their inadequacies. They try everything to get back into the abuser's good graces. They strive to become perfect in every area the abuser wants, yet he will continue to raise the bar on what is expected.

Shame is what keeps survivors going back to an abusive relationship. Outside the relationship shame feels even more overwhelming to victims of abuse. They will drive themselves crazy wondering what people might think. They worry excessively about judgment. Survivors can become consumed with thoughts of what might happen if anyone knew the truth. They are deathly afraid that other people will see what they already believe about themselves. They go back and forth in their minds about what is worse, ending the dream or being judged by their friends and family. They think to themselves, "At least in the abusive relationship I know exactly where I stand," so they remain in it.

On average, abused women attempt to leave their victimizers six to eight times.[2] The abuser will prey on their feelings of shame and use "honeymoon" tactics to lure them back. They will promise to change, reigniting "the dream" in the mind of the survivor.

Survivors become experts at hiding the truth. They build up a fantasy picture in their minds and convince all the people they know that the fantasy is true. They master how to cover up every last detail of the sad truth. They become "perfect."

Shame plays an incredibly important role in this form of perfectionism. I have called myself a recovering perfectionist for years. Releasing myself from the pressure of being "perfect" was a critical step in my ability to release the shame and find self-compassion.

Recognize. Vocalize. Mobilize.

How often do you . . .

Diminish the value of your accomplishments?

Think that you are not enough?

Beat yourself up for decisions you have made?

Dismiss compliments from others?

Blame yourself for things that have nothing to do with you?

Think of yourself as a bad person?

Avoid making decisions because you are afraid of being wrong?

Strive to have everything be perfect?

Then ask yourself . . .

How much longer do you want shame to control your life?

What actions can you take right now to stop shaming yourself every day?

How will it feel when you are not constantly filling your mind with this shame?

Lesson 5

Releasing Fear

"Breathing deeply and releasing fear will help you get to where you want to be."—Iyanla Vanzant

Fear keeps us small. Living with abuse means living with constant fear. Victims fear that they will be abused, but they also fear life outside the sphere of abuse. Paradoxically, abuse becomes their comfort, validating all the terrible things they think of themselves. Their emotions shift to anger or depression.

I skipped many days in high school because I was paralyzed by fear. Sinking into isolation felt easier than going to school and trying to maintain a facade that everything was normal at home. Many children today experience the same fears.

Fear can manifest itself in any number of forms. When men abuse, most often it is to cover up deep-seated fears of losing power, likely as a side effect of power's being taken from them as children. Fear can also manifest itself as mental health issues such as anxiety and phobias or psychological disorders.

People have a subconscious tendency to deny even the feeling of fear. Most experts believe that the key to overcoming this problem is to recognize the fear as fear. People who develop the fears they had during childhood sometimes do not outgrow them, and the fears remain rooted in their psyche, negatively affecting how they interact socially.

Only when people fail to acknowledge fear or acknowledge it too much does it become a problem. Despite being a natural part of the human psyche and survival instinct, fear is often regarded in today's society as something that should be removed. Our media are filled with stories of figures who literally feared nothing and took insane risks. While some fears are irrational phobias, being afraid is not always a negative thing.

Fear triggers the survival instinct that prevents us from taking too many unnecessary risks, whether they be social, physical, financial, or sexual in nature. Fear also prompts the body to enter survival mode when one is faced with extreme danger, pumping large amounts of adrenaline into the system to give people the physical abilities needed to survive certain situations.

The object should never be to get rid of fear entirely. We have it for a reason. Instead, we should evaluate why we have a fear and seek to diminish it.

Fear often presents itself when you ask people why they have not achieved their goals or the level of success they desired. They usually will respond with some built-in excuse (negative belief) that held them back. Underlying this excuse or negative belief is a fear. How many times have you attempted something new, only to stop before you ever got started because you were afraid of what others might think? Or because you believed that you were too inexperienced or lacked the knowledge to succeed?

Fear shows up as well when we have chosen to believe in something that is not really true. Worry is nothing more than a sustained fear caused by indecision. Sometimes we need to ask some tough questions to determine the cause of these worries or fears. The following exercise will give you a framework to identify a fear so that you can release it and no longer permit it to control your life.

Sit comfortably in a quiet place. Relax, close your eyes, and take several deep breaths. Breath through your nose, eventually letting your breathing assume a natural pattern. Pay attention to to the air moving in and out of your lungs. Let the tension drain from your body.

Then ask yourself . . .

What am I afraid of right now?

What am I worried about?

What does fear or worry feel like in my body?

What feelings come up for me as I think about this fear? Shame? Pain? Sadness? Pleasure? Anger? Imagine that the feelings are not me but just passing through me.

What is the worst possible thing that can happen if this fear or worry comes true?

What plan do I need to put in place so that the worst thing does not happen?

What will it feel like to have the fear but not let it control me?

Continue this exercise for each fear that comes up for you. Take a deep breath and notice whether you feel different—maybe less worried or less attached to the fear.

LESSON 6

Overcoming Isolation

"The number one tool of an abuser is isolation."—Author Unknown

Your abuser wants you to be silent. Your abuser wants you all to himself. He doesn't want you to think or dream or live. He will do whatever is necessary to cut off your contact with other people. He will try to convince you of horrible things about your family and friends to separate you from them. He will insist on moving far away from your family and friends to weaken your support system. He will control your phone, your computer usage, and your schedule. He will tell you where you are allowed to go. It is essential for your abuser to use isolation to maintain his power and control.

My boyfriend in college who almost killed me controlled where I was every minute of the day. He would check up on me five minutes after I wasn't with him. He would ask me question after question, sometimes the same question in different ways to see if I would trip up in my answers. He told my friends lies about me so that they would stop being my friends. He embarrassed and humiliated me regularly. All of these tactics were used to isolate me so that he could maintain control.

It can feel impossible to break out of such a situation and reestablish a relationship with family and friends, but it must be done if you are to overcome the feeling that you are alone in your struggle. If you don't want to talk to family and friends first, find someone else—a therapist, a private group, someone.

You must recognize that it is the fear, shame, or sadness that is preventing you from reaching out and getting the help you need. You must learn to believe in the deepest part of your soul that there are people in the world who are ready to love and support you. The fear or shame or sadness you feel has nothing to do with the reality of those who can help you.

Don't make the mistake, however, of reaching out to people who have never supported you before. Make a decision to take the new information that you have learned to guide you to the right people who can help you and love you the way you deserve to be loved.

Recognize. Vocalize. Mobilize.

How has isolation impacted your relationship to yourself?

With which family members and friends do you most want to reestablish a relationship?

How will you feel once you have reestablished those relationships?

Are there people in your life with whom you long to have a relationship but know they are no good for you?

Forgive the people who have shown you that they should not have a place in your life and move on to finding the kind of caring people you deserve.

How can you strengthen or build your support network so that you feel more connected?

After answering these questions, practice the following exercise as you concentrate on gentle, rhythmic breathing.

Tune into your body so that you know when you are feeling lonely or helpless. It's very important to be able to name the feeling, though it may take some time to recognize such feelings if you may have been avoiding them for very long.

Recognize. Vocalize. Mobilize.

Embrace the feelings as you would a child who is hurting. Allow yourself to experience and accept the feelings for a few minutes.

Be willing to release the feelings. Imagine the feelings of loneliness and helplessness moving through you and being released into the universe.

Now imagine that you are surrounded by people who love and support you. Imagine them showing you compassion and love. Feel in your body the rippling of love as they honor and support you.

LESSON 7

Overcoming Perfectionism

"Perfectionism is a 20-ton shield that we lug around thinking it will protect us when, in fact, it's the thing that's really preventing us from being seen and taking flight."—Brene Brown

I call myself a recovering perfectionist. In my unrelenting drive for personal growth, I realized that perfectionism was blocking my ability to move forward. Perfectionism allowed me to avoid feelings of shame and inadequacy. It gave me an excuse for not feeling bad about myself, yet never quite good about myself either.

Perfectionists aren't trying to achieve something great; they're trying to avoid something negative. Perfectionism causes us to waste a lot of time getting things just right. We have constant anxiety that even the smallest error will have significant ramifications. We often lose sight of the big picture because we are so focused on the trivial details. It doesn't matter how good the results are; we are never happy.

I have talked to so many survivors who suffer from perfectionism. Striving for perfection arises from feelings of unworthiness that were magnified during abusive relationships. I believe that perfectionism is one of the primary reasons why victims remain silent about their abuse. They become consumed by shame and will do anything to keep people from knowing that they aren't perfect.

The pressure on women to be perfect is intense. Society tells us that we must be perfect mothers, wives, girlfriends, PTA members, social-club stars, and aerobics addicts. Even in the grocery checkout aisle you are inundated with media messages about the perfect body, the perfect life, and, oh, look at all the women who fell off the pedestal of perfection— let's make sure that they are vilified on the covers of three magazines.

The media have no shame in telling us what to eat, what to look like, how to parent, how to love our partner, and how to love ourselves. A judgmental society can strip you of your ability to listen to your own intuition. Even if you are in a healthy relationship and have a healthy self-concept, these messages can be hard to process, and they often intensify our quest for perfection.

Overcoming perfectionism can release a tremendous amount of pressure from yourself. Talking about it and reaching out to others is the first step in your recovery.

Perfectionists believe they're committed to excellence, but they're actually avoiding feelings of inadequacy. If you discover that you're a perfectionist, practice each day doing something well but not perfectly. It may take a while, but with discipline you'll be enjoying the benefits of excellence rather than the disadvantages of perfectionism.

Recognize. Vocalize. Mobilize.

In what areas of your life are you too hard on yourself?

Are there areas of your life in which you procrastinate excessively, in which the need to be perfect creates anxiety and keeps you from getting started on something?

Do you judge others too harshly?

Are there areas of your life in which you take things too far?

Think about a recent situation in which everything was perfect. What did you gain?

In thinking about that same situation, what did it cost you to be perfect?

What pleasure do you get from being perfect?

How do you feel when you're less than perfect?

How will it feel when you no longer need perfection in every area of your life?

LESSON 8

Identity

"I am not what has happened to me. I am what I choose to become."—
Carl Jung

When I was a little girl, I had hopes and dreams and endless love and
compassion for the world. Again and again I received lessons about how
this endless love could be used against me. It brought a life full of
challenges that made me question who I was, that steered me toward
situations that would break me down and almost kill me.

Out of fear I did what I was told. I became a person I did not like. I did
things that did not feel natural or congruent with the person I was. My
identity became dependent on who I was with. I suppressed my anger,
my sadness, and my spirit so that I could survive, so that I could fulfill
the dreams of my abusers.

Charlie Cardin

In 2007, when I finally made the decision to stop the cycle of abuse in my life, I had to dig out from all the earlier programming. I had to find me again. I had to reconnect to the person I wanted to be. An important step for me was to compose a declaration to my abusers.

Declaration to My Abusers

You tried to break me.

You tried to take my spirit.

You tried to kill the love inside me.

You tried to convince me that I could never be anything without you.

But the fact is that who I am is greater than what you have done to me.

I am greater than the fear that you instilled in me.

I am greater than what you have told me I am.

You cannot keep me here

In this place of being small.

You know this.

You know that the moment I realize my strength

It is YOU who will fear ME.

I have enough love and compassion inside me to heal the world, But I have NO MORE TIME for those who do not want to be healed.

I was put on this earth to use my power to nurture,

To support,

To love,

To show compassion

For those who need it and are ready to accept it.

I cannot live without serving others.

It is what we as women are meant to do—

To model unending empathy and compassion,

To hold others up who cannot hold themselves.

But I cannot serve if I am not taking care of me.

Starting today I will declare my rights and boundaries in this world

Because I know that I cannot give love until I show love to myself,

And even though I believed in you when I should not have

That doesn't mean I don't deserve love now.

You preyed on my love and my insecurities for your own gain,

But I know what you were doing,

And I know that I deserve to be shown the same love and compassion
that I show to others.

I am done with letting your words and actions control my relationship to myself.

Today I stand up for me and for every other survivor,

And I say NO MORE.

No more shame.

No more abuse.

I will get back to the me I was before you tried to break me.

And I will inspire others to do the same,

And I will walk with my head held high that I have faced the fires of abuse

And that I have survived.

Watch me get back to me and show the world what it is

To be a woman who is strong and powerful and inspired.

Just watch me.

———————

When somebody attacks who they think you are, it can feel as though they are actually reaching inside and uncovering your true self. This is especially true with victims of abuse. Shame will trick them into believing what the attacker says because deep down they hold the belief that they are not enough. Even if what the abuser says is completely untrue, the victim will still let it affect her. A survivor's best defense to escape this drama and pain is to decide for herself who she is and who she is not.

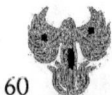

Once I ended the cycle of abuse in my life, I realized how much of my life I had spent being someone I was not. I needed to be open and honest with myself about every mistake I had made that fed into who I was not. It was through this discovery that I learned the truth about who I was and who I wanted to be.

By going through the discovery process of identifying who you are not, survivors can free themselves from the ego attachments that caused them to suffer in the first place.

Recognize. Vocalize. Mobilize.

What have you done in your life that is not congruent with who you are?

When did you let others control your actions?

How does your relationship with yourself need to change?

How much do you define who you are by things that have happened to you?

How do you identify who you are to others?

Does thinking about who you are fill you with joy or cause more suffering?

Recognize. Vocalize. Mobilize.

Here is a simple exercise that can be of help in pondering these questions.

- Sit or lie comfortably in a quiet place. Relax, close your eyes, and take several deep breaths. Breath through your nose, eventually letting your breathing fall into a natural rhythmic pattern. Pay attention to the air moving in and out of your lungs. Let the tension drain from your body.

- Ask yourself, "What defines me?" "What is it about me that makes me me?"

- Sense every inch of your body and know that you are more than your body.

- Think about situations you have been through and ask yourself, "Do these situations define me?"

- Sense a deep connection to who you are and decide that you can be whoever you want to be.

- Let feelings arise as you imagine a new you emerging. Ask yourself, "Am I this fear, this shame, this pain, this sadness, or this anger?" You can see that your feelings are not you. They just pass through you.

Continue this meditation for twenty minutes or so. Take a deep breath and get up, noticing whether you feel different—perhaps less worried or less attached to things, feelings, and thoughts. Repeat the meditation as often as necessary to remind you of who you are and who you are not.

LESSON 9

Visualization

"With every experience you alone are painting your own canvas, thought by thought, choice by choice."—Oprah Winfrey

Every step forward in my life started with a single thought of how I wanted my life to be different. Somewhere along the way I learned about a technique called visualization, which allows one to crystallize a thought and turn it into a full body experience. I think about how I will feel when I have achieved my dreams of who I want to be or what I want in my life. I think about the people who will be around me and how my success in self-realization will affect them. I think about what impact it will have on my community. I know that when I close my eyes and focus on these things, my motivation to accomplish them multiplies exponentially.

It is never too late to make real changes in your life, and anything is possible. If you can think it, you can achieve it. What is possible for you is limited only by your mind and your ability to take action. Below is a simple exercise that can help you to move forward with any change you wish to make in your life and self-concept.

Visualization alone is not enough to accomplish the goal; you must follow it up with action. Visualization gives you the motivation to ensure that you will move forward, and if you use it often it will almost guarantee your success. I am not talking, of course, about visualizing that you won the lottery or will marry a billionaire. I am talking about making qualitative changes in your life over which you have 100% control such as losing weight, advancing in your career, breaking the cycle of abuse in your life, and being a better parent, partner, or human being. You alone have the power to make such defining changes in your life.

Recognize. Vocalize. Mobilize.

Visualization Exercise

Step 1: With a journal or piece of paper in hand, decide on a change that needs to happen in your life.

Step 2: Now write about the following:

- How this decision will impact not only your life but also the lives of others.

- How you will feel once this change has happened.

Step 3: Imagine the feeling of elation as you realize the change.

How will you feel about this change in retrospect when you have reached the end of your life?

LESSON 10

Values

"When your values are clear to you, making decisions becomes easier."—
Roy E. Disney

"Personal values provide an internal reference for what is good,
beneficial, important, useful, beautiful, desirable and constructive."[3]

In the beginning our values are transmitted to us by our parents.
Healthy parents will instill values such as speaking the truth, helping
others, and respecting neighbors. We learn more values during our
formal education. We read about the values of great people and try to
emulate them. Religion also inculcates concepts of right and wrong.
Whatever their source, values guide our behavior in society and at
home.

In order to understand values, we have to understand human nature and human origins. To understand human nature, we only have to look into our own hearts. We know that each of us is capable of positive, constructive behaviors as well as negative, destructive behaviors. The history of mankind, of course, is filled with horrific acts of war, genocide, oppression, and enslavement. However, it also includes remarkable acts of kindness, leniency, mercy, and forgiveness.

Values curb our most terrible behaviors while at the same time encouraging our best behaviors. You can look at them as a sort of coping mechanism that prevented us from destroying each other while we developed as a species.

I had never really thought about my values before I started the journey to change my life. I knew generally what values were, but I didn't understand how important they were to shaping my life and dictating my actions. I set out to discover exactly which values meant the most to me. It was through this process that I learned what I had neglected for most of my life.

When establishing your values, the first thing to keep in mind is clarity. You need to be exceptionally clear about the nature of each value and how it applies to you, your family, and your community.

Next, make sure that your values are formalized. This means that they are not simply jotted down on a cocktail napkin or note pad. The values you espouse are important. Therefore, make sure that they are properly recorded and communicated.

Finally, you need to exemplify the values you embrace. Your behavior will indicate to everyone around you whether the values are real or just a bunch of words. If you are serious about demonstrating the benefits of your values, you have to live them every day.

Recognize. Vocalize. Mobilize.

What are the core values that you would like to integrate into your life?

Why did you pick each of those core values?

How will your life improve by being firmly based on these core values?

How do you need to change in order to begin living these values every day?

LESSON 11

Beliefs

"The outer conditions of a person's life will always be found to reflect their inner beliefs."—James Allen

"Belief is the state of mind in which a person thinks something to be the case, with or without there being empirical evidence to prove that something is the case with factual certainty."[4]

Victims often accept the core beliefs of their abusers without question. These beliefs are reinforced through such intimate relationships. These beliefs then become engrained in the subconscious so that survivors are usually not even aware they are there.

Our core beliefs begin to develop when we are children. They are influenced by parents, siblings, and other significant people in our lives. By the time we reach adulthood, we have developed some pretty fixed opinions of ourselves and the world around us. Once a core belief is firmly implanted in our minds, it can feel impossible to change.

If our core beliefs are, for the most part, positive and empowering, they will be reflected in our attitudes, behavior, and performance. The reverse is also true. If we adopt predominantly negative beliefs, our attitudes and behaviors are severely compromised, crippling our potential for success and happiness.

The question is whether we can change our core beliefs. If there is a recurrent problem in some area of your life, it is usually a good indication that you are entertaining a false or limiting belief. Before a belief system can be changed, however, it is important to understand how a belief system works.

Belief systems are nothing more than ideas that have become so fixed that you don't even notice them anymore. Once established, our belief system will attract the people and circumstances that validate it. As negative beliefs accumulate over the years and become part of the system, it becomes easier to collect "evidence" that appears to support those beliefs and more difficult to see anything to the contrary.

Survivors are conditioned to accept all limiting beliefs implanted by their abusers. These beliefs keep them trapped in the cycle of abuse. The most prevalent is the belief that the abuse is their fault. This misapprehension is accepted because it is a survival mechanism related to "the dream." Accepting this negative belief is easier than confronting the painful truth that their abuser does not care about them.

I fought long and hard to avoid the realization that my father did not love me and was simply using me for his own selfish desires. It was much easier to believe that I deserved his mistreatment. The possibility that he didn't love me brought incredible pain and suffering. I accepted all the negative beliefs that he had implanted in order to avoid the truth.

A big problem arises when we hold onto beliefs even though they may not square with the same situations today. Once you recognize how your beliefs have impacted your life, you can no longer blame someone else for continuing to have these beliefs. Where the beliefs come from is not important. What is important is that we jettison these life-crippling beliefs.

Believe me that you can build a new belief system that will attract the people and circumstances necessary to create the experiences you desire.

Recognize. Vocalize. Mobilize.

What negative or limiting beliefs do you have about yourself?

What beliefs were implanted by your abuser?

How have those beliefs impacted your life?

What are the core beliefs about yourself that you would like to adopt?

What would prevent you from accepting these core beliefs?

How will your life improve after accepting them?

What steps can you take to live these beliefs every day?

LESSON 12

Finding Courage

"Courage doesn't mean you don't get afraid. Courage means you don't let fear stop you."—Bethany Hamilton

When I became pregnant with my son, the event sobered me to my responsibility for his life and my own. I became acutely aware that my own decisions decided the course of my life. I could no longer blame anyone else.

I refused to give in to my fears any longer. These included neurotic fears of rejection or looking stupid; they also involved the fear of commitment, the fear of speaking out, and the fear of facing my truest, deepest desires. The list is nauseatingly long, and I know we've all bought into some of these at least once. These fears have shaped our lives, often to our own detriment and sometimes to that of those around us.

Like the Cowardly Lion, an archetype of the fear-ridden, we need to find our courage. Unlike him, we know that we have to face our fears and find our courage within. Inside each of us beats a brave, fiercely courageous heart willing to take on a challenge if it means that life afterward will be more authentic, happier, and freer. What better challenges to tackle than the fears that have kept us chained to our pasts?

Find a reason to say "yes" today to all the changes that will transform your life, and the lives of those you hold close, for the better. You have only your inner coward to lose!

If you have done the chapter exercises so far, you have gained the knowledge requisite for the courage that any other successful person has. You can now use the power of your beliefs, values, and convictions to confront adversity and succeed against all odds.

I know the courage it takes to leave the comfort of old patterns and beliefs and step into a different life. I truly believe that not one thing I have done or that happened to me defines what I am capable of or how extraordinary my life can be. And I am waiting for you to join me, fire sister, to rise with me.

Every time you feel yourself backing down or playing small, ask yourself what would happen if you went after what you want right now.

Recognize. Vocalize. Mobilize.

Take time to notice how you respond to people throughout the day.

Are there times when you should have spoken up for yourself and didn't?

Are there times in the past when an opportunity presented itself that would have helped you grow but you didn't take advantage of it due to fear?

Are there things that you constantly fear and don't do?

If you did these things, would they bring you more joy or success in life?

Is there any reason why you feel you shouldn't have great joy and success in your life?

What actions would help you to conquer a fear that you have?

LESSON 13

Compassion

"Love and compassion are necessities, not luxuries. Without them humanity cannot survive."—Dalai Lama

Many believe that compassion is directed only at others, but it is much more. My life completely changed when I realized the importance of showing compassion to myself. Self-compassion is the ability to accept our authentic selves without judgment or shame. This is what is required to let go of the need to be perfect. It is what allows us both to honor our values and beliefs and to forgive ourselves if we default on them from time to time. We have to forgive ourselves and process the lesson so that we can be honest about our vulnerabilities to others.

Abuse strips people of their compassion. When people are threatened, they shut down emotionally. Their capacity for normal reasoning and processing become impaired. In many cases the victims are so impacted that they become closed off and may feel that they will never recover even long after the abuse occurred.

Many wrongly assume that once the abuse is over the victim should be fine, but the truth is that the effects of abuse haunt victims long after they have left their abusers.

I felt, and was told, for most of my life that I brought on abuse, and I hated myself for that impression. Every time I got into another abusive relationship I thought that it turned bad because there was something wrong with me. Why did I keep picking these people?

After I had broken the cycle of abuse in my life, I experienced a huge breakthrough when one of my abusers from junior high school reached out to me on Facebook. He explained that he had nearly died from cancer and needed to tell me something, asking whether he could come to see me while he was visiting New England. I listened to my heart and felt compelled to say "Yes." At our meeting he told me that in his moments of near death from cancer all he could think of was the apology he needed to make to me and that he had decided, if he lived, to find me and tell me.

He was the first man in my life to say he was sorry and mean it. He explained the abuse that he had suffered while growing up and how he had taken it out on me. After his confession I experienced a release and wave of self-compassion. I wish I could tell you that I didn't need his apology to feel whole. I wish I could say that I didn't hold on to the effects of his abuse for over 20 years. I had. But now, in the blink of an eye, it was released. I was released from the prison of his abuse.

Suddenly and without warning, I started remembering every detail of every abusive relationship I had been through. All the shame and regret and sadness I had carried for so long, thinking that I had brought it all on myself, I now knew never had anything to do with me. It had always been my abusers' own "stuff" that made them treat me that way.

I had discovered that there was nothing wrong with me. There was nothing wrong with the love I tried to give. There was nothing wrong with showing compassion for others. There was nothing wrong with having hope and believing in the goodness of others.

I started asking myself, "What if the way my father acted toward me had nothing to do with me? What if the way my first husband manipulated me had nothing to do with me? What if the same thing was true of every man who had treated me badly?" While I asked myself these questions, a wave of self-compassion started to flow over me. It was so clear now that it had never been about me.

This realization allowed me to forgive myself for whatever decisions I had made and to free myself from the emotional pain that I had endured all my life. By posing simple questions to myself and having the courage to be vulnerable in conversations, I was able to alleviate a lifetime of pain.

I challenge anyone reading this to dig deep to find the compassion in your heart for you. If you have been abused, compassion will give you the strength to renew your faith in the human race. It starts with being compassionate toward yourself. Give yourself permission to embrace your loving heart fully and without limits. Show yourself the compassion that you show to everyone else. Start right now.

More love + More compassion = More freedom

Recognize. Vocalize. Mobilize.

How often do you beat yourself up for what you have endured?

Are there people you need to talk to in order to clear up any assumptions either of you made?

Do you wonder why you got involved with an abuser in the first place or why you stayed in that relationship for as long as you did?

Are you still replaying messages from your abuser in your own head?

What will it feel like for you to be free of those messages?

How can you start showing yourself more self-compassion today?

LESSON 14

Acceptance and Forgiveness

"Forgiveness means giving up all hope for a better past."—Lily Tomlin

The ability to accept and forgive deeply affects our ability to be in the present. Once a situation is in the past, there is no longer any opportunity to change it. By accepting the past as it was, you can let go of the expectations for it to have been any different. You simply cannot change anything that has already occurred.

I realized the true power of forgiveness when my ex-boyfriend who had cancer came to visit me. He had carried the weight of what he did to me for more than 20 years, and when he was near death the weight of that burden was overwhelming. I knew that I would forgive him. At the time I thought that I was only helping him, but what caught me off guard was the weight that forgiveness lifted from me as well. I realized that the gift of forgiveness is beneficial to both parties and that forgiveness is a choice.

Victims of abuse may feel as though the person who hurt them does not deserve forgiveness. When they do not forgive, however, they continue to hold the weight of the abuse in their hearts. Most likely the abuser has gone on with his life and does not even care about the harm he has caused you. Even so, the survivor can make a conscious effort to forgive.

It is liberating and empowering to forgive someone because doing so frees your mind of negative thoughts. Forgiveness allows you to focus on the positive things in your life and to move on to genuine growth.

I truly believe that our inability to forgive others stems from our unwillingness to forgive ourselves. We believe that we are undeserving of love, respect, acceptance, appreciation, and an abundant life. Somewhere along the line we start to believe that all the rules of the society in which we live define who we are supposed to be. We stopped trusting and believing in our own inherent worth and come to believe that we are "not good enough." We repeat messages to ourselves such as "You failed" to abuse ourselves with shame. These thoughts about ourselves can be more painful than what others say to us.

Shame is deep and pervasive. It involves feelings of inferiority, inadequacy, and being unlovable. These feelings can become convictions about self-worth. Children who have suffered or witnessed abuse often grow up believing they are "not good enough" and become the caregivers for the next generation. And so the cycle goes, on and on.

It is time for this to stop now. It is time for us to accept the decisions that we have made, to forgive ourselves and others who have hurt us so that we can move on with our lives according to our own aspirations.

When your abusive relationship ended, perhaps there were things left unsaid and questions left unanswered. You can use the technique outlined below to have a conversation with your abuser without ever talking to him face to face. You can resolve vexing issues and allow yourself to let go of the past.

Recognize. Vocalize. Mobilize.

Practice Forgiveness

Sit in a quiet place where you will not be disturbed. Ideally have an empty chair or seat opposite you. Close your eyes for a moment, take a few deep breaths, and allow yourself to relax and let go.

When you open your eyes, imagine that you can see the person to whom things have been left unsaid sitting opposite you.

Say to the person whatever is on your mind, whatever you need to release. When you have finished, you may want a response from him. If so, sit in the other chair and pretend you are answering back as he would. Make this projection as real as possible.

When you have finished speaking for the other person, return to your original chair. Keep up the conversation, moving from chair to chair and assuming the other individual's persona until the conversation comes to an end.

This technique is incredibly valuable for letting go of pain, guilt, and hurt from any sort of relationship. You will be surprised by the answers to yourself.

Is there someone in your life whom you need to forgive?

Recognize. Vocalize. Mobilize.

What are your reasons for not forgiving him or her?

Is there anyone in your life whom you routinely derogate?

Has there ever been a time when you hurt someone's feelings and need to apologize?

Is there any festering anger or hurt that you are harboring?

What impact do you think that holding onto that anger or hurt is having on your life?

What would it feel like if you accepted everything that has happened to you and forgave both yourself and others who hurt you?

LESSON 15

Opening Yourself to Change

"Let us not hope for mere chance to change our story; let us summon the courage to change ourselves. Let us believe faithfully that our dreams are worth any struggle and that it is time to free ourselves and rise to glory."—Brendon Burchard

When you have been abused, it is easy to feel that the abuse defines you. Whatever hopes and dreams you once may have had seem lost, and the thought of making changes in your situation can feel overwhelming. I know this fear, and I know what it's like to think that it's easier and sometimes safer to stay where you are. I have spoken to many survivors who get into one abusive relationship after another because they feel that this is just how relationships are. Such thinking, however, is based on negative and limiting beliefs that simply are not true.

Living with abuse was never your destiny, and with over 7 billion people in the world there are almost unlimited possibilities to find a partner who is loving and caring in a way that will allow you to trust again. If you get very intentional and decide on the type of person you want in your life, he or she will appear. But before any external factor changes, you have to change yourself. Accept that is it your own negative and limiting beliefs that are keeping you where you are and decide that it is time to change in order to open yourself to the love and freedom you seek. At any given moment you have the opportunity to decide how your life will be different.

Before I could break the cycle of abuse and create the life of my dreams, I analyzed each of my thoughts, figured out how the thought needed to change, amplified that thought by a motivational factor, and followed it up by intentional action. My motivational factor was my son. Looking into his eyes gave me a fierce determination to make whatever changes I needed to make in my life to ensure that I would never get into an abusive relationship again.

Listed below are the major mental shifts that were critical to open myself to change and create anew my life on my own terms.

Recognize. Vocalize. Mobilize.

Stop blaming others. There came a point in my life at which I had to accept the fact that, although my abusers manipulated me, I still had made the decision to get involved with them and after they abused me had made the decision to stay in the relationships. I may not have had much choice in childhood, but I had a choice later. Once I fully accepted that fact, I forgave myself for whatever bad decisions I had made, and I stopped blaming anyone else for what had happened. Doing so gave me back my power to look at every area of my life and decide what needed to change.

Quit being jealous of others. Jealousy intensifies feelings of the shame of not being enough, and it kept me stuck in making decisions from a negative mindset. I believed that everyone around me had already figured life out. The reality is that not a person on this planet hasn't experienced some struggle or negative beliefs about his or her self-worth. While the people I felt jealous of appeared perfect to me, I discovered as I got to know them better that they had gone through just as much struggle as I had and were just a few breakthroughs ahead of me.

Learn to trust and believe in yourself. Every time I make a decision that is good for me or good for my family, I build trust in myself that I will continue to make good decisions. The better the decisions, the more the trust. The more I built that trust, the more I believed that I could do things that I had never thought of or done before. I started to believe that my life could be anything I wanted

Recognize. Vocalize. Mobilize.

it to be. All I had to do was to believe that I had the aptitude, the motivation, and the desire to learn whatever I needed to learn, find the people I needed to help me along the way, and follow through with action consistently. I learned that the subconscious mind does not know the difference between reality and imagination. That means that I could imagine a life full of possibilities and that, if I worked hard, I could achieve anything.

Find happiness in yourself. I realized that every abusive relationship I had gotten into came about because I was trying to have someone else fulfill my needs. One of my biggest breakthroughs happened when I realized that all the happiness I would ever need was wrapped up neatly inside my own body and mind. I became relentless in my pursuit of internal happiness. I read one personal-growth book after another. I discovered the things that made me feel good such as a hot bath, a walk in the woods, or a ride on my bike. When I accepted the fact that I could create my own internal happiness, my mind starting opening up to new opportunities.

Don't let fear control you. "Daring greatly," wrote Brene Brown, "is being brave and afraid every minute of the day at the exact same time" She taught me that the objective is not to get rid of fear but to be aware of it and push through it. Creating a new way of life with new standards was incredibly scary. Tremendous fear lurked in stepping outside my comfort zone of what I had always

Recognize. Vocalize. Mobilize.

done and forging different relationships. I yet knew that I could not let my fear keep me from having the kind of life that I wanted for myself and my son.

Respect and honor yourself first. Throughout my formative years I had been taught to sacrifice myself to please others. In my subsequent journey I realized that I would be able to help many more people if I honored and respected myself first. I became relentless about establishing my personal boundaries, and I learned how to say "No" for my own well-being and for that of my family.

Believe in humanity. No matter how I was treated or how many times I was abused, I never lost hope in humanity. I knew that I would always be able to find people who were good and honest and true. The greatest way in which I learned this was by volunteering as much as possible. Nothing restores faith in humanity faster than volunteering alongside someone who is passionate about serving his or her community. I volunteered with Habitat for Humanity, Rebuilding Together, StandUp for Kids, and Shriners Hospital to connect with people who exemplified what I wanted to emulate.

Believing in humanity again will give you a stronger sense that you are not alone and that the struggles you face do not have to be faced on your own. You must believe that there is always someone who has faced the same struggles and who is more than willing to help you to the other side.

LESSON 16

Changing Your Story

"The only thing keeping you from getting what you want is the story you keep telling yourself about why you don't have it."—Tony Robbins

I was 11 years old when my father left my mother. My mother and brother were not home, and my father had come home to get his personal stuff. Once he had packed up his van, he asked me to sit down on his lap so that he could explain a few things. He explained how bad his relationship was with my mother and how he had found another woman who was more fun to be around. He cited a thousand reasons why my mother was not good enough for him. He told me that I needed to explain all of this to my mother when she got home because he would not be there and wasn't coming back. I stood in the driveway and watched him leave. I was in shock and disbelief, and I had no idea of how to process the information I had been given.

When my mother returned home, I dutifully informed her of everything my father had shared with me. She was in shock and later that evening had a mental breakdown. Sometime during the night she left us to go get help for herself. My brother and I stayed at various neighbors' houses and then went to stay with my father. It was the first time we met "the other woman." It was a rollercoaster of party after party since my father was in the "honeymoon phase" of wooing his next victim.

The story I had been given by my parents was that abuse was a way of life. Watching my mother be abused on a regular basis made me feel sorry for her, and from as early as I can remember I accepted my role as caretaker. There was an expectation that I would be responsible for my parents yet never better than they were. It was an expectation to stay small so that I wouldn't make my mother feel badly about herself and the choices she had made.

It took me until 2007 finally to decide that abuse would no longer be part of my story. It was then that I realized that nothing in my past needed to define any part of my story. I found that I could change myself and my relationships such that my story would be different. I changed my story by challenging every single belief that I had about myself or my life until that point.

From childhood we tell ourselves many stories as we absorb the environment around us. We accept the mindset of living small because every time we do not succeed we are still praised and accepted instead of encouraged and motivated to do better. At the same time, ironically, our society places many negative connotations on doing well in life. There is a common misperception that those who are very successful are selfish and full of themselves. We become accustomed to thinking that it's better to be just good enough and nothing more.

I challenge you to ditch the idea of living your life by such a standard. When you tell your story, what do you want included in it? Changing your story is much simpler than you might think. You just have to decide that it will be different. That's all. There is no magic pill; you just need to make a crucial decision.

Recognize. Vocalize. Mobilize.

How do you want your life to be defined?

What parts of your story can you release by recognizing that they are in your past and play no part in your life today?

How do you want to live your life in a way that is uniquely yours and on your terms?

Imagine now that you had the life of your dreams. What does your dream life look like and how does it feel?

What actions do you need to take to move forward into that life, a life free from abuse and shame?

LESSON 17

Reducing Negative Thoughts

When reaching out to others and trying to rebuild old relationships or form new ones, you must have an awareness of how much negative energy you are projecting. Being consumed by all the ways your abuser has impacted your life will prevent you from moving forward and keep you from forming positive and fulfilling relationships.

One of the best ways to reduce anger is to not focus on negative thoughts that continue to fuel the fire. It may seem impossible to survivors to remove such thoughts. If the abuser still plays a role in your life, as in shared custody arrangements, there are numerous opportunities to remain stuck in a negative place. Missed court dates, lack of child support, financial pressures—the list goes on and on.

The process of healing will be far more challenging when you hold on to your need for negative thoughts. Their influence is far-reaching, affecting you mentally, emotionally, and physically. There are reasons why pessimists are so miserable.

Here are some effects of harboring anger and negative thoughts in your life:

- It has a harmful impact on your mood and outlook. Thinking negative thoughts can intensify your sadness, fear, anger, and hopelessness. These emotions taint the way you view the world and erode your ability to make wise decisions.

- Negative thoughts inhibit your ability to achieve goals. When you doubt whether you can achieve a certain goal, you're much less able to accomplish it.

- It damages your health by creating unnecessary stress.

- It saps your confidence and energy. Negative thoughts lower self-confidence. Negative thinking can impact everyone around you.

Working to reduce the incidence of negative thoughts is one of the most effective ways to enhance your life. Negative thoughts can undermine your happiness, success, and health.

While you are learning to rid your mind of negative thoughts about yourself, you should also be taking an inventory of the negative people around you. Although it is impossible to avoid negative-thinking people all the time, you can minimize interaction with them by recognizing how they always put a negative spin on everything and make you feel drained after being with them.

Recognize. Vocalize. Mobilize.

When talking to negative people . . .

Do not bring up topics that trigger negativity.

Use redirection and distraction to change topics to something they love.

Remind yourself not to judge or try to fix them. Simply listen.

Avoid making comments that intensify the negativity.

Try to find the good in a situation and highlight that when possible.

Avoid arguments or heavy debates.

Limit the amount of time that you spend with them.

Recognize. Vocalize. Mobilize.

Daily Exercise

Carry a journal with you throughout the day. Every time a negative thought pops into your mind, jot it down.

Think of a positive thought to replace that negative thought and enter it in your journal as well.

Tell the people in your life who love you that you are trying to change this part of your life. Ask them to call you out every time you talk negatively.

LESSON 18

Rebuilding Trust in Yourself

"As soon as you trust yourself, then you will know how to live."—
Johann Wolfgang von Goethe

The most important skill that a survivor must learn to rebuild trust in
herself is to start cultivating and listening to intuition. During their
abuse victims ignore all the signals from their intuition in order to
continue pursuing the dream that their abuser cares for them and will
someday magically return to the honeymoon phase.

Why do some of us seem to have better intuition than others? Perhaps
you believe that you lack intuition altogether. This is not the case. Your
mind is constantly giving you feedback. You're either not receiving the
messages or you're misinterpreting the signs. When you are uncertain

about how to proceed, your intuition can provide valuable feedback. It's a mistake to rely only on logic when you have tools like intuition at your disposal. Give your intuition a chance.

The first step to connecting to intuition is to realize that you already have it. If you've ever had a hunch about something, that was intuition, the ability to understand something immediately without the need for conscious reasoning.

By recognizing intuition you'll have hunches more often. Learn when to trust it. Give it good information, and you'll be repaid with good hunches. This is the simple formula for developing intuition.

Trusting and following your intuition will allow you to take back control of your life. It will make you start doing what's necessary instead of what's convenient.

By listening to, trusting, and following your intuition, you will not get into another abusive relationship. Locked inside you is a vast storehouse of wisdom gained from your life experiences and decisions. Your intuition will utilize that information to guide you if you just listen.

Recognize. Vocalize. Mobilize.

Learn to cultivate and listen to your intuition.

Practice listening to your intuition daily. Start with little things like "Should I go to the movie or stay home?"

How does your intuition communicate with you? Is there a verbal response? Is there a sense of anxiety or calmness?

Start to follow your intuition blindly in trivial matters. Show your intuition that you are willing to listen.

Step outside your comfort level and do something new. Listen to what your intuition is telling you as new information comes in.

Do something that engages your mind at a low level and listen to your ruminations. Your mind will create brilliant ideas while you are driving, walking, or washing the dishes.

Journal about your intuition. Jot down the new things that you have learned about yourself.

LESSON 19

Building Healthy Boundaries

"Givers need to set limits because takers rarely do."—Rachel Wolchin

The most important word to say when building healthy boundaries is "No." If you tend to be a people-pleaser, your inability to say "No" to others can eventually impact your life in a negative manner. If you think back to a time when someone asked you to do something and your intuition said "No" but your mouth said "Yes," how did you feel? You probably felt angry at yourself or at the other person who asked you to do something that you did not want to do. The habit of acquiescence to others' wishes can lead to self-frustration, reduced self-esteem, and depression. It will cause negative thoughts, conflict within yourself, and an overwhelming sense of lost control over your life.

An inability to say "No" more often arises from not determining our personal boundaries and how they will guide our social interaction. I also believe that establishing healthy boundaries is one of the most critical yet least taught life skills for children today. This deficiency is especially evident in families living with domestic violence.

If someone during my childhood had talked to me about the importance of healthy boundaries, I would have known that something was wrong with my family situation. Boundaries would have given me a compass to determine my rights as a human being. Instead, my boundaries were never defined and, hence, never respected.

Setting boundaries can have a tremendously beneficial effect on the following areas of your mental and physical well-being:

- Respect. When you clearly indicate your boundaries, others will have more respect for you; and when they honor those boundaries, you will have more respect for yourself.

- Honor. Having strong boundaries will display your moral character and set the tone for mutual respect.

- Integrity. Boundaries will ensure that you remain true to your authentic self.

- Trust. Building a standard of trust in yourself means that you will not sacrifice your boundaries, drawing more people into your life who can be trusted.

- Love. You will know what you need to feel loved and thereby feel comfortable in showing love to others.

- Compassion. The security of boundaries promotes compassion for others still struggling for acceptance.

- Empathy. You will be able to support others in their experiences without sacrificing your own emotional well-being.

Pay close attention to your intuition when you are asked to do things that encroach on your personal boundaries in any of the above areas. I encourage to go through the exercise on the next page every time you say "Yes" when you should have said "No."

Recognize. Vocalize. Mobilize.

Think of a recent situation in which you said "Yes" when you should have said "No."

Which of the seven areas enumerated above were impacted negatively when boundaries were crossed in that situation?

What do you think made you say "Yes"?

Forgive yourself for allowing your boundaries to be crossed. Make a decision not to let them be crossed again.

If you faced the same situation again, how would you respond differently?

How will it feel when you trust yourself enough to respect your personal boundaries every time?

What needs to change so that you trust yourself to respect your boundaries more?

LESSON 20

What Is It Costing You?

Do you feel stuck? Do you struggle with withdrawal, low self-confidence and self-worth, lack of energy, inability to focus? Or are you just stressed and tired and overwhelmed? Does the thought of making significant changes to your mindset and in your life feel overwhelming?

I know the feeling of wanting your life to be different but thinking there are too many things that have to change. If you do the work to break through a negative mindset, however, your life will improve bit by bit and day by day,

The more you dwell on what is wrong in your life, the more what you don't want will appear. With every negative thought that enters your mind, you need to ask yourself one question: What is this costing me?

In the seconds you spent on doubting yourself, you could have lifted yourself up. In the seconds you spent on feeling sorry for yourself, you could have found at least three things for which you are grateful.

It takes only a few seconds to change your mindset. Think about this: in every moment you have a choice. If you practice asking yourself "What is this costing me?" your mindset will shift. And the more your mindset shifts, the more you will feel the weight of struggle lift, giving you the space to allow more brightness, joy, compassion, and love to enter.

Recognize. Vocalize. Mobilize.

Close your eyes and imagine what your life would be like if you didn't tell yourself that you are not good enough or strong enough or skilled enough or happy enough. Imagine that the internal conversation changes and you start saying things like the following:

I have all the strength I need.

I am listening to my body and giving it all the nourishment and care that it needs.

I am taking the time to connect to myself and the people I love because I know the value of connection.

The world is filled with people who love and support me.

What are the messages that you need to soothe your soul and know that you are being compassionate to yourself?

I encourage you to write those messages down, stick them on your bathroom mirror, and read them several times each day.

LESSON 21

Finding Your Tribe

"Set your life on fire. Seek those who fan your flames."—Rumi

Centuries ago women prepared meals together. They raised their children together. They talked, connected, and could depend on each other. Many of the problems in today's society are due to a lack of deep connection.

A powerful synergy happens when women who love and support each other bond. If you have ever been to a support group with other survivors of abuse, you know this feeling. Finding your tribe is about figuring out how to connect with others and feel a sense of belonging. When you find your tribe, you discover that others fully accept you for who you are, whatever emotional baggage may be encumbering you.

Once you have this level of connection with a group of women, it will totally change your outlook. I feel fortunate throughout my life to have found other women who loved and supported me. These friendships gave me the strength to continue my journey. A woman who accepts you unconditionally when you are at the lowest point in life is someone you should treasure. I would not be here today had it not been for those women who built me up, buoyed me when I was weak, and honored me with their friendship.

If you do not have women like this in your life, there is no better time than now to find them. There are a thousand different ways to find them—support groups, church organizations, parenting groups, social clubs, and business networks, among others. There is an entire tribe of women out there waiting for you to join them. Finding such peers is a critical step in your personal growth and will give you many opportunities to practice your courage and show your vulnerability. If one group doesn't feel right, go to another and possibly another until you find one you can call home. It is by reaching out that you will gain the deep power of connection, and it will lessen your need to have an abuser fill that void.

Recognize. Vocalize. Mobilize.

What type of friends do you want to have in your life?

Where do people like that hang out?

What actions can you take today or this week to bring those people into your life?

What will it feel like to be surrounded by a diverse group of people who love and support you?

Lesson 22

Planning Your Independence

"As one goes through life, one learns that if you don't paddle your own canoe, you don't move."—Katharine Hepburn

I learned the value of independence early in life as I watched my mother struggle emotionally and financially after my dad left us. It was then that I resolved I would never depend on any partner for my financial well-being. Before building my professional career, I put myself through college, working full-time and having a part-time babysitting service while going to school full-time. It took a great deal of persistence and tenacity, but I knew it must be done if I was going to achieve success.

Having my own career and interests always gave me a space that made me feel safe. It allowed me to know that I could depend on myself to do whatever it took to take care of me. Despite whatever challenges I had in my personal relationships, I knew that by continuing to excel in my career I would always have a fallback framework. I would not have been able to end my first two marriages as swiftly as I did without a stable job and an amazing support network of family and friends.

I have talked to many survivors who left their abusive situations with their kids and no money, no clothes, and no other resources. In these situations, they weren't thinking about independence; they were thinking about survival. Getting themselves and their children safe was the priority. But once they were out and safe, it was time to figure out how they would support themselves.

No matter what situation you are in, taking steps to establish or strengthen your independence will have a tremendously positive impact on your life. It will fuel your self-confidence and put you one step closer to stopping the cycle of abuse in your life. Think about each area of your life where you need a greater level of independence.

Every change you make will boost your self-confidence and increase your chances of staying out of relationships that are no good for you. Gaining independence is about realizing that you should never be tied to just one person, one job, or one situation in order to feel connected and whole. Humans are by nature social beings. Find the things and people that bring you joy; do what you need to do to take care of yourself and your family.

Step-by-Step Plan for Independence

1. If you are unemployed, contact the unemployment office or local hiring agencies first. Get yourself something temporary to tread water (and relieve stress) until you can figure out a long-term

plan. Temporary assignments get you back in the game quickly, and there are generally a wide range of jobs available to be filled.

2. If you are already working, are you doing something aligned with what you are really good at? If not, consider a job change to develop your strengths further. You will perform better and likely make more money.

3. Research jobs that pay at least as much or more than what you need to make. Figure out which ones align with your strengths and write down what additional skills you may need to acquire.

4. Evaluate your skills and strengths. Plan a schedule to round out your skill set for the job on which you have set your sights. Contact organizations that offer training in the skills you need. Look at community colleges in your area that offer free training in various areas. Also look at online courses, many of which offer scholarships depending on your financial situation.

5. Don't be afraid to seek jobs for which you may not yet have every specified skill set. Trust yourself, and persuade prospective employers, that will be able to master these skill sets on the job.

6. Find networking groups in your area to meet people already working in the same positions you want. Ask them tons of questions about what gave them the most success in their fields and what they recommend for someone just starting out.

7. Evaluate your debt, create a budget, and talk to a financial advisor. Many such advisors will do an initial analysis for free. Establish goals for where you would like your finances to be in a month, year, and three years.

8. Find a hobby about which you are passionate and connect with similarly inclined people. Give yourself permission to have a little fun.

9. Renew your commitment to self-care. Exercise, meditate, take a hard look at your diet, and give up things that are hurting you physically and mentally.

10. Every time you make a significant change, celebrate the fact that you are moving your life forward. If you try and fail the first time, pick yourself up and tackle the change again. Understand that nothing worth doing is ever easy.

The decision to make a positive change in your life can be exciting and terrifying at the same time. All of the changes noted above can be contemplated before you ever leave an abusive relationship. Give careful thought to the changes you want to make. Think through the end result, and prepare for anything that could happen along the way. Make conscious decisions and heed your intuition. You will know when the time is right to make a change. Trust yourself.

The decision to make changes in your life is yours and yours alone. They should feel right and good to you. If you are still in an abusive relationship, make changes carefully and safely without alerting the abuser. Remember too that nothing in your past defines what you are capable of.

If you were strong enough to live with abuse, you are more than strong enough to remove it from your life and live abundantly. Start making plans to build your independence today.

Recognize. Vocalize. Mobilize.

Of the ten steps identified above, which ones do you need to take now to plan your independence?

How will it feel when you have gained the independence you desire?

How will this independence help you, your family, and your community?

Get out a calendar and set dates for achieving each goal you set for yourself.

Commit to taking action every day toward realizing each of those goals.

LESSON 23

Building Self-Confidence

"The only person you should try to be better than is the person you were yesterday."—Author Unknown

Put simply, self-confidence is belief in yourself. Sometimes you are your own biggest enemy, especially when you allow your fears and self-doubt to sabotage your success. A critical step to achieving the seemingly impossible is to realize that the answer already lies within you. Not giving up and trying again will give you the confidence that you can overcome anything you set your mind to.

If you start changing your mindset to believe that struggles in your life are just opportunities to learn more and to challenge you, you can surmount them all. The more struggles with which you are faced, the easier the process becomes. Your confidence is self-perpetuating by nature, meaning that with each success comes more success.

The most important step you can take in building self-confidence is to present your authentic self. Abandoning perfectionism and unrealistic expectations can help you to settle into who you are. Living out your values and beliefs consistently will reinforce your ability to honor and trust yourself, breeding even greater self-confidence.

When you are living authentically, you will no longer need the approval of others. You will no longer feel compelled to change yourself to fit the mold prescribed by other people. Obsessive desires to please will melt away. Abusers try to convince you that your authentic self is unworthy and will never be enough. Building self-confidence starts with rejecting everyone else's idea about who you are.

Some basic character traits build self-confidence and, if adopted, will be stepping stones to gain the success that you desire.

Perseverance. Successful people don't give up on their dreams. By persevering through emotional discomfort, you will teach yourself that you can overcome any obstacle. Perseverance also promotes stability and consistent progress. Keeping your goals in mind consistently will keep you pushing through adversity.

Reliability. The more that you show yourself to be honorable, the more that reliability will become part of your character. This will attract other reliable people to you and strengthen your current relationships. Others will know that you will do what you say and that they can trust you.

Optimism. You will bring more good things into your life just by believing that they will come. When you expect the worst, you often receive the worst. Optimism relieves stress and promotes well-being. It allows you to see the best in a situation instead of the worst.

Courage. Fear can be a good thing by challenging you to do things that you otherwise would not do. If you push on despite the fear, you will experience a greater sense of accomplishment, giving you the necessary confidence to keep tackling those fears one after another.

Self-Discipline. If you discipline yourself to take at least one step every day toward realizing your dreams, your progress will grow exponentially in no time! Every step you take will make it easier to take one more step.

Generosity. When you're willing to give part of your time, money, and attention to others, the positive energy you generate will come back tenfold. Don't limit your generosity. Give as often you can and release the need to tell anyone about it. Tony Robbins has a saying that "If you don't give when you have nothing, you won't give when you have everything."

Self-Awareness. If you become aware of your thoughts, actions, beliefs, and values, you will know when you are stepping out of your authentic self. Once you have this awareness, you will always have a choice of deciding on future directions in life.

Humility. By staying humble, you will serve more, achieve more, and be more. Humility gives you compassion for other humans and keeps you focused on striving to serve authentically and honestly.

Curiosity. A healthy curiosity about your feelings, about others, and about life in general will keep you searching for answers and pursuing the path to personal growth and learning.

Recognize. Vocalize. Mobilize.

Which of the character traits listed above would you like to strengthen?

What steps do you need to take to start strengthening those traits today?

What are some situations in your life when you have been prone to low self-confidence?

How did your personality, opinions, and level of honesty change during those times?

What will it feel like once you have gained self-confidence in all of these areas?

Lesson 24

Breeding Positivity

"The mind is everything. What we think we become."—Buddha

One of the best ways to attract more positive energy into your life is to let your own positive energy shine through and be a light unto others. Your life will dramatically improve if you become more positive in your thoughts, words, and actions. One of two things will happen to the people around you: either they will become more positive in turn, or they will show you that it is time to lessen their impact on your life.

Abusers are by nature negative people. If you become a strong and positive force, you will repel them. If you do the following on a consistent basis, you will become more positive in outlook.

Show others that you love yourself. Model how you want others to treat you by treating yourself that way first. Don't put yourself down in front of others. Treat your body with respect, eat right, drink alcohol in moderation, and model to others how to respect your boundaries.

Treat others the way you want to be treated. The more you demonstrate respect, honor, and trust to others, the more they will treat you the same. Model your best and authentic self no matter how others treat you. Know deep inside that if someone treats you badly, you will recognize the boundary that has been crossed and send them on their way out of your life.

Accept yourself as you are. You bring special gifts to the world. The more you accept your strengths, quirks, and limitations, the more others will accept them. Accept the fact that who you are and what makes you different from everyone else is interesting and that anyone who doesn't seem to think so doesn't deserve your time and effort.

Get happy. Trent Shelton once said, "There are 150,000 people in the world that die every day, but today you are not one of them." Use the opportunity you have been given to enjoy life to the fullest. The more you smile, the more others around you will smile.

Do not talk badly about anyone. The more you focus your energy on the good in life, the more you will see good things happen. Spending your time and energy on talking badly about anyone or anything will create more negativity in your life. Make a decision today that you will not say one negative thing about another person or situation.

Practice gratefulness daily. No matter what your situation, there is always something for which you can be grateful. Starting your day by thinking of at least three things for which you are grateful will get your mindset into a state of abundance that will carry over to the whole day.

Recognize. Vocalize. Mobilize.

When during the day do you catch yourself being negative?

How can you make those messages to yourself more positive?

Are there negative people in your life with whom you need to spend less time?

Are there people in your life that you need to influence to be more positive?

How will it feel when you are surrounded by positivity?

LESSON 25

Practicing Self-Care

"I have come to believe that caring for myself is not self-indulgent. Caring for myself is an act of survival."—Audre Lorde

Taking care of myself was one of the hardest skills to master when I was overcoming the effects of abuse. I had a lifelong pattern of sacrificing my financial resources, personal safety, beliefs, values, and health for others. Time after time I was left depleted physically, emotionally, financially, and spiritually. When I broke the cycle of abuse and started taking care of myself, I started to experience feelings of joy that I had never known before.

The joy came from my ability to forgive myself and let go of the need to be a people-pleaser and perfectionist. I no longer needed those patterns to cover up my feelings of not being enough. I no longer needed to devote myself wholly to my career, sacrificing my health in the process. I started to experience life in a whole new way.

Part of my self-care development was in allowing myself to be fully present with my kids. Their laughter and love of life continue to be a gift to me. In experiencing them, I learned the true value of enjoying the little moments of life.

I know that it can feel scary to take care of yourself the way you need to. I know the demons inside us that tell us we don't deserve to feel good and look good. I have talked to many women who can't even get out of bed or take a shower because they are paralyzed by the shame of abuse.

It's time for this to stop. It's time for survivors to start enjoying life. The only way in which they will be able to have the freedom they desire is by taking care of themselves first.

If you are a survivor, make yourself get out the door and begin experiencing the life you deserve. Begin by calling friends or joining a group of people. Practice being fully present in every experience. Try to reserve a time during the day to go window-shopping, walk in the nearest park, or exercise at a gym. Those precious moments away from it all will refresh your body and mind.

You must stop thinking that doing what you need to do in order to take care of yourself is a luxury. Instead, you should think of it as the time necessary to charging your batteries and energizing your life's purpose. Others' expectations, as well as your own, can be a heavy load to carry around 24 hours a day, 7 days a week. Below are some self-care tips that can get you started on your journey to strong mental, physical, and emotional well-being.

Consistently plan your future. What do you want your life to look like in a year? Two years? Ten years? What type of person do you want to be by then? What impact do you want to make on your family, your community, and the world?

Evaluate what you are eating and drinking. Cut down on sugar and white starches. Focus on eating whole-grain, high-fiber foods, fruits, and vegetables and on drinking plenty of water.

Find work/ life balance. People spend more time on work than they do on any other activity except sleep. If you are spending more time than you should at work or if your job makes you miserable, everything else in your life will suffer. Money isn't everything. You must find time to do the things that inspire and recharge you, that make you feel as though you are truly living. What are the things that you love to do that you never take time for? Schedule them and stick to your plan.

Get some sleep. Studies show that your body requires at least 7-9 hours of sleep every night in order for your cells to regenerate properly. Your ability to manage stress, make smart decisions, and regulate your emotions depends on getting enough sleep.

Increase your self-awareness. Notice your thinking patterns throughout each day. Notice your feelings. Notice your habits, needs, desires, strengths, and weaknesses. If you wish any of these were different, take action to make the change.

Spend time with positive people. Do the people around you mirror your own positive thoughts, actions, and values? If they don't, find people who do. Look at networking groups or find a cause and volunteer your services. Make worthwhile connections!

Spend time with your tribe. Your mental and emotional health won't be optimal if you spend time only on work. We all need to experience deep connections to others, especially those of like mind, to achieve good mental and spiritual health. Find a tribe that you love and nurture those relationships regularly.

Train your brain. Find some hobbies that keep your brain challenged. Learn how to play Sudoku or learn a musical instrument or another language. Cut down on sugar and caffeine intake, and consult your doctor on supplements such as fish oil that will help your brain.

By giving careful attention to each of these areas and making positive changes in your life, you will improve markedly in self-confidence.

Recognize. Vocalize. Mobilize.

In what areas of life do you need more self-care?

What is stopping you from making these changes in your life?

How will you feel when you have incorporated more of these changes in your daily or weekly routine?

When will you start making these changes?

What do you need to put in place today to start these changes?

In what ways are your negative beliefs about yourself sabotaging your self-care?

LESSON 26

Reconnecting to Your Body

"To me, beauty is about being comfortable in your own skin. It's about knowing and accepting who you are."—Ellen Degeneres

I completely disconnected from my body every time I was abused. I felt alone and confused, and my intense shame made me hate my body. It was a vicious circle. Having developed early, my body made me an object to the wrong type of people. I felt bad about myself and was so starved for love that I gave my body to abusers in hopes that they would show me any kind of love. Every time subconscious messages would scream that I should surrender because it was all that I deserved. My internal programming for disconnecting from my body was strong, and I could not get past it until I became pregnant.

When I felt my son growing inside me and saw him on the ultrasound, everything changed. I began to look at my body as an amazing creation. No longer was it defined by my abusers. I finally accepted my body as my own and decided that I would never allow another person to disrespect it. For the first time in my life my body was my own, and it was beautiful.

I discovered that touch was so much more than what is involved in sex and abuse. I discovered an amazing love and beauty when I touched my son's face and he touched mine, when I held his hand, when he stroked my hair. I had never experienced unconditional love like this—no expectations, no control, no shame, no guilt. I understood now that touch wasn't supposed to be frightening.

I explored this newfound discovery further by working with massage therapists. I learned not just the power of loving touch but also the power of love. I learned how to feel present in my body and to appreciate it.

Sometimes all it takes is to remind the universe of what you are willing to accept and it will respond. I made a decision to love my body. Heavy or slender, short or tall, young or old—this body is what allows me to experience life, to hug my children, to love my husband, to help heal others.

I now have tremendous gratitude for the vessel that has carried me through life and allowed me to give birth to my children. It continues to allow me to learn and grow and share and love.

Recognize. Vocalize. Mobilize.

Do you need to reconnect with your body?

What beliefs or feelings do you have about your body?

What steps do you need to take to heal your feelings so that you may love your body and experience loving touch?

What would it feel like to enjoy your body again?

What would it feel like to experience loving touch by someone?

What boundaries are important to you about touch, and what would you be willing to explore?

LESSON 27

Creating Healthy Relationships

"Vulnerability is the birthplace of connection and the path to the feeling of worthiness."—Brene Brown

In order to have a meaningful relationship with someone, you must have the courage to be vulnerable. I believe that learning how to start and nurture relationships is one of the least taught skills today. Most people apply what they have learned from their childhood, which is often inadequate and especially so if they grew up in an environment of domestic violence. I also believe that most of the suffering in the world today is the result of the inability to develop a deep connection with other people.

Lack of connection drives us into meaningless and sometimes dangerous relationships. We may get involved in a relationship to stop some kind of pain in our lives such as loneliness. Our pain clouds our judgment, and we miss all the warning signs of abuse.

When I broke the cycle of abuse in my life, I was determined to overcome the pain of loneliness. Some of my darkest days came during high school when I didn't get out of bed for days on end. I associated being alone with all that pain, and I continued to get into whatever relationship came along to avoid it.

When I made the decision that my life was going to change, I knew that learning how to have a healthy relationship with someone had to start with my relationship to myself. I had to learn how to love my own company. I learned that I didn't need another person to fill a void or enhance my life.

My concept of relationships changed completely during that time. I no longer looked for friends or relationships to complete me, for I now knew that I was complete all by myself. I learned that I was enough. For the first time in my life I started being selective about who I spent time with. I gravitated to people who made me laugh, who inspired me, who loved me for the person I was. I learned the power of deep connection and how to seek out truly meaningful relationships.

Below are some lessons that I think are critical to both starting and maintaining loving relationships with people who are worth your investment of time and energy.

Be intentional about who you want in your life. My inability to decide who I wanted in my life kept getting me into dysfunctional relationships. When I sat down and made a list of what the people in my life should be like, those people started coming my way. It really is that easy. You just have to decide.

Realize that no one can read your mind. Others cannot guess your needs or opinions. If you don't make your desires known, you should not expect to have them met. Take the first step in satisfying your needs by sharing them clearly. A brief talk each day can avoid unnecessary drama and relieve anxiety.

Argue with compassion. If you're going to argue, take into account the other person's point of view. Stop what is coming out of your mouth and don't say anything until you understand the other person's position. Don't try to win just to be right. Talk about their behavior instead of attacking who they are. Avoid such generalizations as "You always" and "You never." Just as you must show compassion to yourself, you should show it to others.

Avoid making assumptions. You will continue to struggle with friendships and romantic relationships if you make too many assumptions. Sometimes people do and say things that have nothing to do with you. Stop letting your ego take over and ask for clarification. The only assumption you should make in any situation is that there is a harmless explanation until you learn otherwise.

Believe that people are doing their best and that they have good intentions. No one can give you his or her best every minute of every day. They all have their own lives and their own challenges. Relish every moment they share their life with you.

Stop expecting a relationship to fulfill all of your needs. We each have our own needs and desires, and no one person should ever be expected to fulfill all the needs of another. Instead, fill your life with people who inspire you in different ways so that you may continue to grow as an individual.

Be the friend, partner, or parent that you wish you had. Be supportive and positive and engaging and joyful. Stay in touch; do the right thing; be there when they need you; forgive them and love them despite their faults. Surprise them; delight in them; honor them; respect them. Model your beliefs and values, discuss the differences, and decide to enjoy those differences.

Be present with them. The greatest gift you can give someone is to be fully present with them. Being genuinely interested in someone can establish instant friendship and build a long-lasting relationship. Listen to people in your life. Try not to think about the next thing to say. Just listen.

Recognize. Vocalize. Mobilize.

What are the characteristics of people you want in your life?

Do you have those types of people in your life now?

If you don't, where can you find them?

If you do, what can you do today to celebrate them?

Are there people in your life who could use a little more support?

When can you call or visit them to show that you care?

CHECKLISTS

15 Early Warning Signs of Abuse

Learning these early warning signs of abuse can save your life.

1. He asks questions that make you feel uncomfortable. He invades your privacy, reads your emails, and examines your phone.

2. He controls your time and prevents you from connecting with those you love.

3. He puts down your friends and family.

4. He picks on you for things that you may already feel bad about, exploiting your weaknesses.

5. He doesn't have healthy relationships with a diverse group of people.

6. He brags about how badly he treated another person in a previous relationship.

7. He does not respect your body and forces himself on you.

8. He is not liked by most of your friends.

9. He asks you to do risky things such as unprotected sex, heavy drinking, and drugs.

10. He is intensely jealous of close relationships you have with other people.

11. He tries way too hard to win your affection.

12. He treats restaurant servers and retail associates badly.

13. He gets furious when something embarrassing happens.

14. He treats his parents poorly and has unreasonable expectations of them.

15. He doesn't listen to you, cuts you off, and talks about himself most of the time.

If you have noticed one or more of these warning signs, chances are that they indicate a dangerous relationship and that you should move on immediately. You don't owe the person anything.

5 Ways to Protect Your Children from Dating Violence

One of the things you need to make sure of as a responsible parent is that your child understands the possibility of dating violence. This is becoming an increasingly common danger for young people today. As a matter of fact, statistics indicate that one in three teens will encounter some sort of violence during their dating experience.

Although you can't completely protect your kids, there are many things that you can do to educate them and help them avoid this type of situation in the first place.

1.   Talk to your children even before they reach the teenage years. Do everything in your power to let them know they are wonderful human beings and give them the strength and self-confidence to stand up for themselves. Always keep the lines of communication open so that your teens know that they can come to you with a problem and won't be chastised or made to feel foolish just because they made a mistake. This isn't a guarantee that your daughter or son won't fall in with the wrong type of person, but you'd be surprised at how much your belief in them can help them make good decisions even when you're not around.

2.   Explain to your children what is considered appropriate behavior and what isn't. For example, when someone is dating the school "jock" she may think it's romantic if he is overly possessive or jealous. Make sure your children know that there is nothing romantic about that type of behavior. Review the early warning signs of abuse in this book so that your teenager knows how to spot abuse. Other forms of behavior that often can escalate into physical violence are mockery, manipulation, and flirtation with others. Basically bad behavior of any sort should be considered a danger sign, and your child needs to know that

if she sees any of it in a dating relationship, especially in the beginning, she should stop seeing that person right away.

3.   Discuss date-rape drugs with your children and what impact such drugs can have on their judgment.

4.   Let your children know that they will meet mostly good people and they don't have to go through life feeling afraid. Just let them know that if a person or a situation doesn't feel right it probably isn't and that they should trust their intuition while being alert to warning signs.

5.   Teach your children about the dangers of peer pressure and the importance of standing their ground for what they know is right despite being made fun of. It is critical for them to develop the skill of saying "No" in order to follow their intuition and maintain their personal boundaries.

Protecting your child from dating violence is something about which every parent needs to be proactive. The best thing you can do for your children is to raise them with a strong sense of appropriate versus inappropriate behavior and the self-confidence to distance themselves from anyone who doesn't have strong moral character.

8 Ways to Help Survivors You Know

1. Listen to them. Survivors need to feel that they can talk to someone they can trust.

2. Show compassion. Domestic violence happens regardless of race, gender, or income level. Know that it can happen to anyone, and do not blame or reject the survivor.

3. Validate. Help the survivor understand that she is not alone and that she is not to blame.

4. Research options. Victims of abuse know the best path to survival, but they may not know how to find people to help them. Research options in your area and let the survivor know where to go and whom to contact for help. The telephone number of the National Domestic Violence Hotline is 1-800-799-7233.

5. Show up. Survivors need to know that when they are ready to make a change they will have people available to help and support them.

6. Model healthy boundaries. Don't push survivors. Don't invade their privacy. Support them unconditionally.

7. Exercise with them. Encourage them to get outside and go for walks with you. Go for a run or a bike ride. The exercise will help them to clear their head, and the fresh air will calm them.

8. Check in often and call 911 if necessary. Don't be the friend who thinks someone else might do something for the survivor. If you sense imminent danger, call 911 and report it. You may save the victim's life.

8 Ways to Help Children Amid Abuse

1. Provide for them. Experts note that babies and older children who have their needs met consistently—needs for food, comfort, attention, etc.—are learning the message that they have worth. It can be hard when you are going through abuse to give children the special attention they need, but it is critical if you want them not to continue the cycle of abuse.

2. Have fun and play. Children learn about and interact with their world through play. Your children idolize you, and playing with them will give them a sense of wonder and joy.

3. Be present and interested in them. If your children receive the message that they are the source of your stress, they may begin to accept that impression. They will see themselves as an annoyance, undermining their self-confidence.

4. Watch what you say. Don't talk in front of your kids about your relationship problems and try to shelter them from the abuse. They will sense what is going on, but exposing them to it will almost guarantee long-term detriment. Do your best to be honest about the situation in a way that your child is old enough to understand. Young children will just get scared, so you need to protect them.

5. Don't withhold love. If your child makes a mistake, assign appropriate consequences but always follow it up with love. Withholding love sends the message that your child's achievements are more important that the child him/herself. Make sure that your child knows you love him or her no matter what failures happen. This does not mean that you as a parent need to accept constant failure or not encourage your child to do better. The important thing is for your child not to think that your love is conditional. Privileges can be conditional; parental love shouldn't be.

6.   Assure children of your love. The most important thing you can do to combat their fear is to show them often that you love them unconditionally. The best way to show them love is to spend quality time with them. Remember that they want your time, not your things.

7.   Let them process their emotions. Teach them that it is okay to have a range of emotions about stressful circumstances but that those emotions do not have to control them.

8.   Get them safe. If your intuition is telling you that you are not safe, your children are not safe either. The longer you stay in an abusive relationship; the more damage will be done to your children's mental well-being. Start making a plan to get them safe.

10 Steps to Safety

---

1. Locate all important documents: ID cards, health insurance, birth certificates, bank records, mortgage agreements, social security cards, etc.

2. Plan to leave when you are confident that your abuser will not be around.

3. Safely store electronic passwords and change them if possible.

4. Keep a cache of medications, glasses, money, family keepsakes, and clothing.

5. Make a list of numbers for the local police department and shelters.

6. Secretly notify family members and friends of your plan, emphasizing the need for not alerting your abuser.

7. Contact a lawyer and discuss divorce and child custody. Become familiar with your rights.

8. Compile evidence of threatening texts, phone calls, conversations, and physical violence.

9. Do not inform your abusive partner of your plan.

10. Start a pattern of leaving the house for longer periods of time.

Conclusion

"The fastest way to change society is to mobilize the women of the world."—Author Unknown

Many people who hear my story wonder how I survived. The adversity in my life taught me courage, strength, and resilience. It taught me the value of compassion, especially to the self. It also taught me how to appreciate the good times and to find joy and beauty in special moments.

Friends from my childhood while all this was happening now ask why I didn't know at the time. People don't realize the shame and isolation that come with abuse. Survivors don't want other people to know the circumstances. When they have an opportunity to go out with friends, they just want to forget.

I was attending a personal growth seminar called High Performance Academy in 2015 when I met a woman who worked in a domestic violence shelter. After I shared some of my story with her, she told me how it could help other survivors reclaim their lives after abuse.

Later that night I realized that I could no longer be silent about what I had gone through in my life. I realized that it was my responsibility to assist other victims of abuse in their struggles, to support them and let them know they are not alone, so that they can be the women they were always meant to be. Within a few short months I founded Fire Sisters Rising, LLC.

Throughout my corporate career I had made it my mission to mentor women in realizing their full potential, but now I had an even deeper mission. I now know that everything that happened to me was so that I could be right where I am today. I could have taken a different path. I could have been resentful and angry, but that would have robbed me of the gift of this moment to bring hope to others.

I challenge you to think of what you can be grateful for today. There will always be struggle in life, but that doesn't mean that it has to control you. Nothing in your past defines what you are capable of or the amount of joy you deserve. Accept the fact that you have the power to do anything you set your mind to and move forward despite your fear.

Every day you have an opportunity for your life to be different. Make a decision that your life will no longer be just about survival. Decide today that you can have the life of your choice. Open your mind to the possibilities and start taking action toward realizing your dreams.

It's time to break free from the cage and start living again. Break the silence, get yourself safe, and make the decision that your life will no longer include abuse. It is time to surround yourself with people who can help to heal you, inspire you, and help you grow. It is time to change the beliefs that have kept you stuck where you are. Dig deep and find the innate courage to do what needs to be done for yourself and your children.

You are not defined by the actions of others. Who you are and who you will be is not defined by this moment. You have a chance right now to rise above your challenges. Break free from those who try to keep you small. If you were abused yesterday, you don't have to be abused today. You can heal these wounds; you can have a different experience. Close your eyes, listen to your heart, and breathe.

Know that you are not alone. Open yourself to love and support others. When you do, love and support will come back to you abundantly. You just have to be open and believe. Love is not a scarcity in this world, but our openness to accept it is. I have discovered time and time again that when the right people are in my life, they honor me and love me despite whatever struggles I have faced.

Can you feel us here waiting for you, sisters who have walked through the fire just like you? We have felt your pain, and now we need you to find your hope and your courage and join us on the other side in a life of freedom and joy. Find the reason that will motivate you to rise and join us on the other side. We are waiting.

Endnotes

1. Centers for Disease Control and Prevention. Retrieved September 2016.
2. "Building Futures: Domestic Violence 101." Building Futures. Retrieved September 2016.
3. "Personal Values." Wikipedia, Retrieved September 2016.
4. "Beliefs." Wikipedia, Retrieved September 2016.

ABOUT THE AUTHOR

Charlie never has and never will let her past define what she is capable of, instead she charges on and sets her sights on new heights every day.

Amassing over twenty-five years working in corporate settings, Charlie Cardin decided to jumpstart her own business, Fire Sisters Rising, to spread awareness, ignite feminine power and instill confidence in survivors of abuse. A survivor of abuse herself, Charlie has devoted her career to helping women to recognize, vocalize and mobilize in order to put an end to the cycle of domestic violence.

As a Certified High Performance Coach, Parent Leadership Coach, Professional Speaker and Domestic Violence Consultant, Charlie's unique areas of expertise allow her to help women transform their lives who are ready to overcome the effects of adversity in their lives and become an unstoppable feminine force.

Charlie is accredited through the Project Management Institute, and is a member of the National Speakers Association and Women's Speakers Association as well as Toastmasters International.

Charlie was recently awarded 2016-17 National Association of Professional Woman of Year.

Thanks for reading!

Please add a short review on Amazon

and let me know what you thought!

Connect with me on social media:

www.facebook.com/FireSistersRising

www.twitter.com/CharlieCardin

www.instagram.com/firesistersrising/

Connect with me through email:

Charlie@FireSistersRising.com

Find out more about my programs and coaching:

www.FireSistersRising.com

www.ingramcontent.com/pod-product-compliance
Lightning Source LLC
LaVergne TN
LVHW021456080426
835509LV00018B/2298